A Hidden View
Images of Bahia, Brazil

A Hidden View
Images of Bahia, Brazil

edited and translated by
Amanda Hopkinson

Frontline / Brazilian Contemporary Arts
publication sponsored by West Merchant Bank

Acknowledgements

The publishers would like to acknowledge the assistance of Bob and Moo Broughton (Viva Brasil), Bud McLintock of Karen Earl Limited, E Crepaldi for the use of her photographs, Jan Brown for her time and commitment, and the sponsorship of West Merchant Bank Limited in the production of this book.

Brazilian Contemporary Arts would also like to thank the following for their help and support: the Governo da Bahia; Organizacão Odebrecht; Petrobras [Petroleo Brasileiro SA]; Varig international airlines; London Arts Board; London Borough Grants Committee; Visiting Arts; and the Brazilian Embassy [London].

First published in Great Britain, 1994

Frontline States Limited, 41 High Street, Barkway, Hertfordshire, SG8 8EA

Brazilian Contemporary Arts, Palingswick House, 241 King Street, London, W6 9LP

Copyright © Amanda Hopkinson, 1994

ISBN 1 873639 04 X

A Hidden View: Images of Bahia, Brazil has been published to accompany the exhibition held at the Barbican Centre's Concourse Gallery, London, from 26 April to 16 May 1994, as part of Brazilian Contemporary Arts' 1994 Festival of Bahia.

The other photographers participating in the group show courtesy of the Cultural Foundation of Salvador de Bahia are: Aristides Alves, Mário Bonfim, Christian Cravo, Francisco Diniz, Vito Diniz, Mush Emmons, Rogério Ferrari, Adenor Gondim, Isabel Gouvêa, Arthur Ikissima, Saulo Kainuma, Gilberto Melo, Dario Guimarães Neto, José Queiroz, Sérgio Rabinovitz, Roberto Rego, Carlos Rizério, Bauer Sá, Arlete Soares, Alba Vasconcelos

Designed by Jan Brown Designs, London

Printed and bound by Balding + Mansell, Wisbech, England

Contents

Preface

A 'hidden view' is the look of the insider, whose presence can safely be ignored. A view that is almost impossible for a visitor to achieve. It is also a view that is most often kept hidden, perhaps because it is in the interior of the country, off the beaten track of its coasts and cities. Or because it's of a way of life lived according to its own norms, perhaps for a long while in clandestinity, something with a reason for being separate, if not secret. The vision, then, depends on who views, what is viewed, and the relationship between the two.

How it's received is determined by you, the viewers. There is no single way of reading these images, many of them mysterious to our ways of seeing, none of them seen here in Britain before. Whether created by a born *baiano* or a foreigner who has, through the years, been adopted by this unique region of northeastern Brazil, each view is taken from the inside. Each aspect illuminates something beyond the tourist beat of beaches, markets, colonial squares and Carnival sambas. In Anna Mariani's case this has literally meant reiterated journeys into the interior, documenting the sparse scrubland of the backwoods and the scattered houses, still oddly designed according to the tradition of early Dutch settlers and painted with a blend of pastel delicacy and robust humour. Just as the Brazilian literary classic *Rebellion in the Backlands* lent inspiration to her fascination with the interior, so her work lends a fresh power to a reading of Euclides da Cunha – or Mario Vargas Llosa who based his *War of the Worlds* on the same backlands, the same possessed visionary.

Miguel Rio Branco is an established photographer and film-maker, an unusually un-photojournalistic member of the Magnum agency. His flawless sense of colour, whether in subtle shades of monochrome or in vivid off-primary colours, owes much to his dual career as a painter. Increasingly, he exhibits largescale painting alongside his often abstract photographic images.

At the same time he has frequently taken a shrewd look at groups often marginalised by the rest of society: boxers at a gym in downtown Rio; street children around the Candelaria church where the 1993 killings took place; the whores of the colonial quarter of Pelourinho, Salvador. (Salvador being the capital of the state of Bahia and, until the nineteenth century, of all Brazil. Hence the writer Jorge Amado's reference to it in the Introduction as the country's 'first and principal' city). His 'hidden view' is that of someone whose presence has become an accepted part of the environment, one that in turn endows a caught corner of cloth or the shadow of a lintel with as much meaning as a carefully-recorded portrait.

Mario Cravo Neto is a portraitist with an historical memory. While Brazilians are generally loathe to divide individuals into 'black' or 'white' – and often laugh at attempts to do so, since we're all varying shades between – there's an obvious reason why Bahia has also been known as 'little Africa'. In the course of over three centuries (Brazil being the last country to formally abolish slavery in 1888), up to ten million blacks were displaced from their countries of origin. Their subsequent history is built into the structure of the city they largely built themselves, with its wealth of gilded baroque churches and convents, the picturesque narrow houses with their wide wooden gates and ornate balconies. The very name 'Pelourinho' at the centre of Salvador city, means 'pillory' or 'place of punishment' for those slaves determined to rebel or run away.

Cravo Neto's image of a naked man hung upside down is a collective memory of that time. 'Collective' also because he works in collaboration with his subjects, so that together a doubly-powerful portrait is created. Alongside collective memory there is the personal: the man who is now a house-painter was a fisherman, relishing the heavy slither of cool wet sea-mackerel down his back. The mingling of memory with having a mind to the future is there in the portrait of a friend with AIDS, eyes looking inwards, pressed shut by a metal sculpture, anticipating the coins placed there after death. Finally, there are those memories at once collective and personal, part of a continuing tradition referred to by Cravo Neto's mentor, Pierre Verger, when he writes: '… the slave ships transported across the Atlantic not only the bodies of captives … but also their personalities, their ways of behaviour, as well as their beliefs'.

These beliefs, specifically in the form of the Afro-Brazilian religion of *candomblé*, are the springboard for Cravo Neto's most imaginative portraits. They are also the substance of Verger's own work as an ethnographer and photographer, now going back over sixty years. Having started as a photojournalist in the early 1930s, in the hope that the work would lead him to travel, Verger discovered that the place and time of our birth is a matter of complete happenstance. Although European in origin (he did not discover his German and Belgian roots until recently, having always assumed he was 'merely' French), he has led a chameleon existence in an astonishing variety of countries and cultures. Nonetheless his spiritual home is with the religions of West Africa, whose adherents he has faithfully – lovingly – recorded both there and in Brazil. That renders him, he believes, a particular kind of a 'messenger' between the two, in which photography has been but one instrument of communication.

Carybé is another foreigner, of Verger's generation, who arrived at Salvador de Bahia from Buenos Aires in 1950 – and found himself unable to leave. His artistry ranges across the spectrum of sculpture, carving, oils, watercolours and sketches and is likewise rooted in the African belief-system that itself took such fertile root in this region of vast plantations and hidden wildernesses. His eye is not that of a dispassionate observer but of a committed initiate able to communicate to the rest of us what we might otherwise not have the eyes to see. After all, it's too easy to visit Bahia's quaint museums and unspoilt beaches without cause to wonder at what might be hidden from view…

Each of the photographers discussed their ways of seeing in their home surroundings, in some cases followed up with further interviews at my home in London or when we met up in Paris. France has traditionally been more welcoming to artists from Latin America. Hence the fact that while all those included have shown there – and, often, also in Holland and Spain – almost none of their work has previously been on public exhibition in Britain. While these four chapters are the outcome of lengthy edited discussions made, as we have been trained to do for the records of the British National Sound Archives, with as little intervention and questioning as possible, the chapters on the two mixed media artists have been compiled from a variety of sources. We have been happy to welcome their work to this collection through the generous assistance of Robert and Mairin Broughton and Edna Crepaldi of Brazilian Contemporary Arts. Luiz Figueredo adds a sparkling exuberance and (I hope he forgives me for saying it) joyful vulgarity to the proceedings with his vivid proliferation of mermaids and madonnas, paintings and tapestries, serpentine sculptures and dancing decoration. My thanks to them all.

Amanda Hopkinson
March 1994

Introduction

Jorge Amado

This is an exhibition worthy of those who would like to learn something of our *baiano* reality, controversial as it is, with its human poverty and perpetual beauty, seen with a special perspective – Bahia, the first and principal land of Brazil. This exhibition highlights, with others, the art of three photographers working here: Miguel Rio Branco, Anna Mariani and Mario Cravo Neto.

I'm well aware that Miguel Rio Branco wasn't actually born within the State of Bahia. He's the son of an important diplomat, born at Las Palmas in the Canary Islands, which doesn't render him in the least degree less of a *baiano*. Any more than the eminent ethnographer-photographer Pierre Verger, though born a Frenchman, is any the less *baiano*, by dint of his artistic creation drawn from the spirit of the *baiano* people.

Raised a *baiano* under the twin wings of love and friendship, he also evokes the face of Bahia reflected in the most exact image of our people, in his well-established body of photographic images. Leafing through them, my attention pauses over the lad with one leg raised like a *capoeira*[1] blow; at the Bar Oliveira, in the district of Rio Vermelho, there are the two mulattas, an older and a younger one, the mixed *baiana* race in all its splendour; not even the most miserable poverty can succeed in clouding its grandeur. Miguel Rio Branco, the artist, his gaze penetrating through his camera, plunges into the depths of life, reaching its most dramatic borders, the lives of the whores, and exposes them to the light of humanism. I call Miguel *o senhor fotografo*, a great *baiano* photographer.

The same feelings overwhelm me when I again pore over the view of *baiano* life illuminated by another master of photography of no lesser significance. His name is Cravo Neto, my 'nephew' Mariozinho [little Mario]. He was born here in the city of Bahia, to the wedding bed of Lucia and Mario Cravo – he the sculptor of christs and *exús* (messengers of the gods).[2] For this reason, and because I've followed his growth as an artist since his earliest efforts, when he was still hovering on the threshold between sculpture and photography, Mariozinho effectively grew up to be my nephew. He decided in favour of photography, in preference to simply carrying on his father's tradition, and he decided well. Today Cravo Neto, with an international reputation, honours and represents Bahia.

I would also mention a *baiano* surrealism in talking of Cravo Neto. His recreative life is not restricted to recording the reality immediately around him, he multiplies and divides it, he increases and diminishes it, in a game of truth-telling in which all things are fused. And so he delineates this tropic by stripping the human body and capturing the beating heart within. Just a few days ago, I was deeply moved to see Mariozinho's portraits of his inventive father, courageous mother and romantic friend Ramiro Bernabó, son of the painter Carybé.

To complete this initial trinity, there is the photographer Anna Mariani: this Christmas I received the present of her book of *Façades* and that on the semi-arid *sertaõ* (backwoods). These go beyond the magical city of Salvador da Bahia, beyond metropolitan man, living between wretchedness and festivals, far beyond all these and into the *sertaõ* of the scrubland where live both hermits and bandits, and where villages dwell behind their coloured façades, poetic façades.

Anna Mariani leads us along paths taken by Antonio Conselheiro and we penetrate the realm of the *latifundios*, those vast estates of wealthy landlords and lowly servants, a land of cracked and hostile soil where only the strongest survive. But, as the author Euclides da Cunha taught us, *the backwoodsman is a strongman* and holds onto life tenaciously: one day the rebellion in Canudos will eventually emerge victorious and the fruits of the earth will belong to us all.

Away from this dramatic, often cruel, but always beautiful scrubland, we are transported through this indigenous artform on a human scale by Anna, shepherdess of the backwoods, bringing home the lyricism of the little houses in the little provincial towns and villages, their pretty façades painted in the pastel shades of a delicate palette. For there are no greater artists than those who paint the walls of the poor homes of the Brazilian interior, of the Brazilian northeast.

Thank you, Anna Mariani, for being the artist you are. You made me proud and happy, and I consider sadly how your father, my late but unforgettable friend Clemente Mariani, can now never share in this contentment. I would have to cover many pages in order to relate all that Clemente Mariani accomplished for the art of Bahia. I'll limit myself to saying that Anna, his daughter, has gone beyond his excellent standards of good taste and culture in order to recreate, with extreme sensitivity and strength, the *baiano* backwoods and the little houses, the man-made houses. How beautiful they are!

In considering the next two contributors, my sole possible reason has to be that of pride in looking back and thinking that perhaps *I* did something for the land of Bahia, our land, its soil and its sky. The reasoning behind this vanity is twofold, linked to both science and art. It concerns the disembarcation of two eminent citizens at Bahia, two of those who together have done most to make Bahia what she is, reconstituting her memories, restoring her to life. The man of science has the greater seniority in years: an ethnologist, historian, wizard. The artist is the younger of the two, a master of drawing and water-colour, a painter and sculptor, a sprite, a devil.

Pierre Verger, a name out of the French aristocracy, also called Fatumbi, a name out of black Africa, out of the kingdom of Oyó, Ojuobá in Bahia. Verger studied and revealed the umbilical cords linking Africa and Brazil: the traffic in slaves; the sagas of the *Orixás*[3], the African and the Brazilian rites of *candomblé*[4], their similarities and differences, the science revealed by divinations and the use of herbs, the mystery and the mingling. One day the French nobleman abandoned his own, his weapons and coat of arms, his insignia of nobility, and slung his camera from his shoulder to travel the outside world. His photographic undertaking, from China to Cuba, from Thailand to Haiti, the portrait of the Brazilian interior in the 1950s, is without comparison. Greater even than that of the scientist, of the French Doctor of Scientific Research, the colleague of Roger Bastide, the *babalaô* Fatumbi, Professor of Ifa University in the kingdom of Xangó; specialist in African studies at the Federal University of Bahia, Ojuobá at the shrine of Opô Afonjá, raised by the venerable Mother Senhora.

Pierre Fatumbi Ojuobá Verger sailed to Bahia because he read the French translation of my *Jubiabá*, also called *Bahia of all the Saints*.

Born in Buenos Aires of an Italian father and Brazilian mother, Héctor Julio Paride de Bernabó – too much of a name for an artist, though a good one for a tango singer: Julio de Bernabó, the Divine

Bandoneón, the unlucky gambler: Héctor Paride, *el Papito*, he abandoned them all to call himself Carybé – he wandered high and low in search of a homeland, painting the high Andean goats, crossing the pampas on horseback in a red cap and poncho to catch his Nancy – and captivate and capture her he did – then one day came upon and read *Jubiabá* in Spanish translation and embarked for Bahia.

As soon as he landed he started painting panels to commission for Anísio Teixeira, Edgard Santos and Clemente Mariani, clothing the city in arts and character. During Opô Afonjá, Mother Senhora touched his head with a blade; Mother Meninha do Gantois bestowed her *adja* into his keeping; Oxossi commanded him to draw, paint and sculpt, recording the city and its people, in memory and in life. He recreated the whole of Bahia, and from his hands grew mulattas, fishermen, the *capoiera*-dancers, the whores – in engravings, in watercolour, in sketches, in oils, and the *Orixás* carved in wood are in the Museum of the Black, born of the handiwork of the hammer and chisel. Carybé wed himself to Bahia in a mutually fertile relationship.

So I bestowed both a wise man and an artist upon Bahia and this is no mean feat. Should I or shouldn't I therefore have grounds for pride? Perhaps it wasn't really I who brought them over the frontier of mystery and into Bahia. Perhaps, rather, it was Father Jubiabá [hero of my book], for whom Gilberto Gil composed a song and Nelson Pereira dos Santos made a film. Jubiabá, priest of the African saints, a saintly father of the city of Bahia of All Saints.

Here I shall cease my praise of this exhibition and its artists. I wish to explain nothing more, simply to remind you that it was with Bahia that Brazil began. It is here, too, that our country's two greatest truths – syncretism and the mixture of races – were conceived and nurtured. *Axé*.[5]

1. *Capoiera*: African martial art disguised as a dance under slavery.
2. *Exú*: messenger of the gods, similar to the Greek god Hermes, but deliberately confused by Christian missionaries with the devil.
3. *Orixás*: the African gods transported in the slave-ships and deliberately confused with Christian saints to keep their presence hidden.
4. *Candomblé*: the practice of Afro-Brazilian religion.
5. *Axé*: a force of spiritual energy; an expression of greeting.

Translated with additional assistance from Lucia Villares

Mario Cravo Neto

Clyde Morean
1993

My name is Mario Cravo *Neto*, which means grandson: I'm the third generation with the same name. My grandfather was a businessman and he didn't want my father to become an artist at all, just to stay a businessman like him. So my father had to struggle to fulfil his dreams and do something he really loved. First he trained as an astronomer, an interest that seemed to be born of a teenage obsession with Flash Gordon, his trips to the moon and the rest. Then, after a period of study in Rio, he decided that all that had too much to do with mathematics so he decided to be a sculptor – he was already very skillful with his hands. But the background in astronomy gave a certain strength and energy to his art, and you see from looking at the sculptures all that they have to do with the cosmos.

What it gave me was an artistic environment to grow up in, here in Bahia, something I'm very happy about. In 1964, when I was around seventeen years old, we left Salvador for Berlin. The Ford Foundation and the Berlin Senate sponsored my father to move his studio there for a year, along with other artists, musicians and actors from around the world. It gave me the opportunity to mingle with artists as diverse as Igor Stravinsky and Herbert Read, as I would help out my father, preparing drawings and so forth. In 1969 I moved on to the United States, and managed to stay out of both English and photography schools. Whatever I learnt, I picked up from watching others work. Experimentation is the most important lesson, it teaches you not to become dependent on only one medium, only one style.

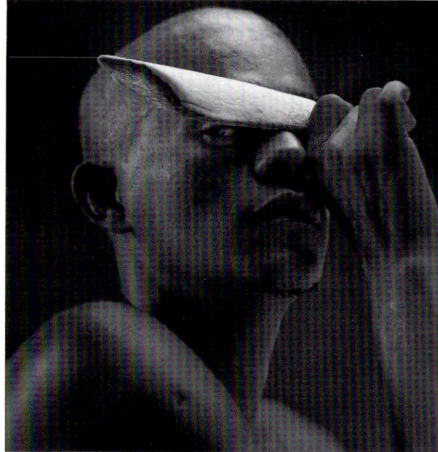

I read an enormous amount, without wanting to adopt a particular school of working. That stuff about being influenced or not by another artist, another photographer, it's a kind of a joke. I've seen similar work by artists from any part of the world who have no contact with one another. Sometimes there are certain ideas that are just 'in the wind' but, more than anything, artists simply draw on what comes from inside themselves. This is of far greater influence than anything which comes from outside. Perhaps it's to do with archetypes and our interpretation of them…

When I went to New York, aged twenty, I simply wanted to gain new experiences, use new materials. I was doing a lot of sculpture at the time. Living in a big city was a lesson in having to abandon all contact with nature. By way of compensation, all the sculptures I was experimenting with at that time started to have to do with nature, using terrariums filled with organic plants. (Did you know that terrariums were actually invented in England, at a time when gas lighting killed off any attempts at keeping house plants alive?) Of course as soon as I got back to the tropics I didn't feel any need to keep working in this way. I was also already taking a lot of black and white street photography.

Tinho with bone
1989

That was the way I worked for many, many years. The only thing that changed my technique to studio-based photography was a car accident in 1974. Everything in life becomes very simple when you use the good and the bad things alike, always to move in a new direction. After the car accident I had to spend a year in bed, without moving, and afterwards I could hardly walk around being a 'street photographer'. I stuck to the black and white, however, for although I'd done some work in colour – and really enjoyed it – it was very expensive to get Cibachrome and to process it here. There's much more control if I keep it all close to home: here, I can shoot in my studio and print in my own darkroom, one next to the other.

Angela and Lucas' torso with dog
1988

The first photographs I took in the studio were much more straightforwardly to do with portraiture. I arranged my own backdrops, natural light, studies of faces and bodies. Very Irving Penn. Now I'm using strobe, all kinds of artificial studio lights, it's again a matter of experimenting in techniques that happen to be new to me. It permits me more flexibility, particularly in using live animals in the ways I now do in my work. Rather than have to manipulate natural light through a fibreglass screen I can have the freedom to capture the image I want in far less time, no waiting around to catch the light, and far less aggravation to the animals. All my models, animal and human, I know. They're all from around here, literally or metaphorically part of the family. I don't use commercial models. There's not even any particular reason for a wide variety of models: I can create better simply by knowing someone better.

It's the antithesis of documentary work, which in any case I find very dated at the moment. Photography just deals with creativity. Now that I'm more skilled in the tools I'm using I can go back to taking photographs in the street without being over-concerned with 'capturing reality'. What I'm trying to catch through my lens, however, is not realism but something closer to a painting, a sculpture, or a poem. There's an element of photography that's always documentary, that's a constant. All that means is that a photograph is a two-dimensional version of something taken from life. Not even the tools matter very much and I don't want to advertise my cameras!

What does matter is the mind behind them: the pictures could be created just as well through digital imaging as by conventional printing. In my opinion, taking traditional black and white film, printing in silver – as I do – is absolutely no different to operating a computer-linked digital camera and a laser printer. Value resides in their artistry, not in the technique that's used. Interpretation is restricted to the theme, context and the result. If I could move the subjects around different media and apply my own original concepts, I'd be happy to. I'm not particularly attached to the format I'm using for its own sake.

Every artist's wish is to communicate, firstly with their inner nature, then to the viewer, then into the future. I happen to use the tools that seem to me appropriate for this. My conclusions are very simple, it really doesn't matter what response I get to my pictures, for we can't really know how profound that is, nor how a picture might affect someone into the future. I don't really consider other people's possible reactions when I'm working, I'm too busy with my own side of things. In any case, an adverse criticism can sometimes help you to get better results another time.

It's important for artists to be able to live by their own work, and it's not possible to ignore the fact that viewers are necessary. Inevitably this kind of work leads to hard times, but it also leads to rewards. The balance you have to strike is in keeping success from interfering in your creativity. Not that photography is in a box of its own: I could just as well be discussing it with people in other branches of the art world, and usually do. Photography is still a very new discipline, it's not properly regarded as just another form of artistic expression. On the whole I prefer to show my work to poets rather than fellow photographers.

What counts most is the living example of parent to child. Often artists' children have a really hard time, all kinds of family politics, but in my family we all tend to show and discuss our work with each other. I'm the only one of four children to have turned out artistic, and that was something that started young. The worst punishment I could be given – I would have had to have been really naughty for this – was to be forbidden to go to my father's studio for a week or more. My temper, my temperament is probably more like my mother's but she didn't practice as an artist. That is a very difficult area to pronounce on, a woman who has babies as soon as she's grown up. Living with an artist is hard work, it takes a lot of energy, creating a family background. It's hard to say who is and isn't an artist in that situation. Now I'm married to Angela, also an artist, and she's going through a rough time in her work, combining it with two small sons. I also have two other grown-up children, a daughter who has moved from Denmark to study fashion design in Paris – that's a really suspicious profession in my opinion – and Christian, who is another photographer! He is young, only twenty, still a purist.

Occasionally I take on commercial work to subsidise my creative work, not very often and I try to work within Brazil. Fortunately the commissions are very free, more a matter of contributing my private work to fill someone else's brief, often photographing art objects or paintings. But occasionally I do fashion shoots, and last year there was a Pirelli calendar I did some

Write
1992

shots for here in Bahia, in which I adapted my own sort of style to colour imagery.

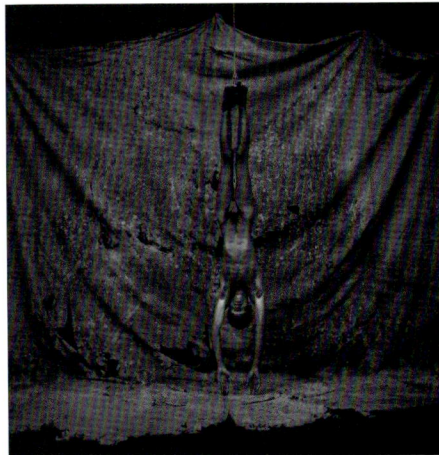

Pelourinho 1989

I also made a trip to Luanda to photograph sixty-nine sculptures from the Angolan Museum of Anthropology. I had to transport an entire studio as there is absolutely no infrastructure to work with there, and of course three crates of materials went missing on the way over. Given that I only had a week to complete the entire assignment, I was not pleased to be kept waiting around. But I completed the job and, since there are few proper publishing houses here in Bahia, a construction company published the work as their yearbook. In the end it all turned out fine and I enjoyed the experience of working in a different way.

It probably resulted from the fact that the first book I did like that was back in 1983, when I was asked to do one on my father's work. He was also originally self-taught, though later he studied in Europe and the United States. His work was very much informed by *candomblé*: he was very close to other artists of his own generation like Carybé and Rubem Valentin, Geral do Carvalho, and learnt from his own *santero* teacher. You can't grow up here and not be affected by *candomblé*. No, it's not frightening at all. I wish there could be more possession, more trances! Possession for me is all about dreams, and it's important to have all that brought into your life. Creating a book from someone else's work is very different from simply taking your own photographs: you have to learn another person's artistic landscape.

This led to a book on *ex votos*, votive offerings traditionally left at wayside shrines by way of petition for the restoration of health or happiness. They're carved and painted by local people, sometimes crudely, sometimes with great beauty. Look at the wooden foot in this picture here. It could be that the guy never had time to finish the piece, or that he wanted to show how he was suffering, the skeleton almost poking through the foot. What an achievement to incorporate the rough bark of the wood as a form of skin disease! It's a plea for sympathetic magic and a genuine form of religious art. Like Cubism, these *ex votos* have African roots, but you can find manifestations in European art from the baroque to the modern age. Going to Angola, I saw very similar, equally beautiful pieces.

There followed a book about Bahia I was very disappointed in because of the quality of the printing: I was learning from my mistakes, all the problems of layout and so forth. There are few trained publishers here and I was busy learning from experience. I had to do it all from square one, finding someone to sponsor everything including the film and print costs. Almost the only way to publish here is by going to one of the major banks for sponsorship or by self-publishing, which is what I did. With hyperinflation around 40% a month, any arrangement you reach over paying for design, graphics and the rest also changes monthly. It's a truly crazy system. And books come out incredibly expensive: a thin paperback novel costs easily $30. The books are all assignments over which I had little control.

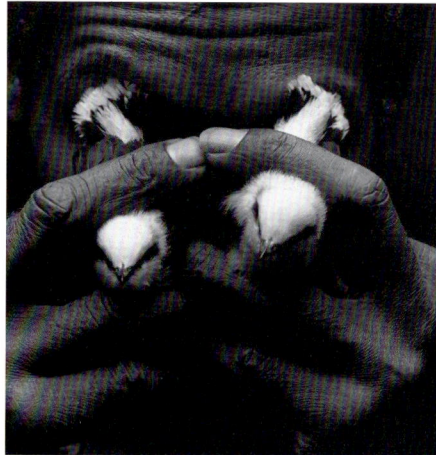

Man with bird tears 1993

So, there's a lot of going back to first principles and acquiring new skills. Or perhaps that sense is intensified by having lost everything I'd first created – all my artefacts and my negatives – when we moved from Europe to the United States. Several trunks went missing on the way over and I lost all that early work I'd done in Germany and Italy. Everything. Now I try and travel more within Brazil, but even that isn't so easy, in a country as big as North America! At the same time, there's a fair bit of Europe here in Salvador, within the artistic community.

For example, one very influential person is the Frenchman Pierre Verger. He has a very long story, he's a photographer, of the same generation as Cartier-Bresson. He is one of the foremost authorities on African influences here in Bahia. He has no phone number because he leads a very simple life, without the communication systems of the modern age. He's an old man, in his nineties, and an old friend. He was probably my first contact with photography. In the 1950s, when he first moved to Bahia, he kept all his prints and negatives in my father's house. Even now, he still lives in a very humble little

place, in the slums at the edge of town, off the road.

His story is that he was born an aristocrat, he came from a very grand French family. When his parents died he inherited and then he surrendered everything. The family had founded a paper factory for fine printing, and he rejected the whole thing to go and discover a new world. He travelled and took photographs and became as significant in his own way, I believe, as Cartier-Bresson or any of the other big names of his generation. In his youth he called himself a photojournalist, but when he came here and started documenting Afro-Brazilian culture, it turned into something very different, very special, very creative. He's the only person who ever photographed what related to *candomblé*, because he's part of it all, he's a *pai de santo* because he had to become involved, incorporated: he couldn't just stay outside of it all. At the same time he still travels to and from Europe, he spent many years living in Africa – he's an example to us all!

The kind of work I now do bears little relation to that early influence. A show at the Fisher Gallery in Los Angeles a couple of months ago depended on us creating a large installation, with two Hasselblad projectors turning over about a hundred 5x5 metre images accompanied by sound. Unbelievable quality, fascinating to work on. All were in black and white apart from one colour image of an eighteenth

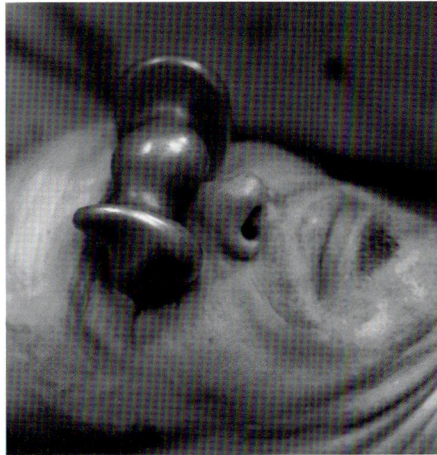

century wooden statue of the crucified Christ from a convent here in Salvador. It's a Foundation for the Arts Project we've been doing for three years now, changing theme every year.

What's happening now is that the majority of photographers using nude models, whether men or women, link their work closely to the erotic. In my case my models are naked because my reality in the tropics is naked. It's simply a different view of the world, very rooted in what I live here and what I found out in Africa. One of the women I was working with in the museum there was pleased to pose with the dagger, the instruments, of the Queen of Angola. This model is another friend of mine, it was in the *Nudes* exhibition at the Nafoto international photography festival in São Paulo last year. This *vodun* man, as he's called, of course refers back to our African religion but it's also quite simply a childhood memory of the black bodies of men who every year whitewashed their houses and got spattered with paint. The way they looked was a visual pleasure to me, and I linked that to my knowledge that *vodun* participants paint their bodies like that. It remains one of my favourite pictures, *candomblé* and *vodun* are like two different but related West African religions.

There's another one I did afterwards when, with the warmth of the man's body, the whitewash started running and streaking. Another where I decided to swop a certain imagery around: traditionally, under slavery, black women had to wet-nurse white babies. In my picture there's a whitened woman exposing her breasts to a black man standing, his back to the viewer, in the foreground. It's a very simplified way of looking at an intricate question. Blacks transported as slaves came from around 800 different African peoples, yet almost all who were brought to Bahia – and to Cuba as well – came from Benin. It's pointless talking about their religious traditions if you happen to be visiting Angola or Mozambique and expect people there to understand. On the other hand a martial art like *capoeira*, disguised under slavery as a dance, is quite independent of *candomblé* and is common in Angola. For me the most important thing is that, over 500 years, a religious syncretism has allowed African beliefs to be kept intact. But they are mixed with the Portuguese *confrarías*, the Catholic fraternities that participated in the Holy Week processions.

Our *baiano* heritage is a common theme of my photographs. This one of the man hung upside down relates to Pelourinho, the name of the colonial town centre of Salvador, where the slaves used to be brought for public punishment. Hanging a man upside down was retribution for his running away. The stretched canvas is a tarpaulin I found on an old railroad in the countryside, something I've used for wrapping my sculptures, and as a studio backdrop.

The sculptures themselves, or lumps of unused clay, also tend to get incorporated. Plus anything else, scrap metal and tyres, old ropes and sailcloth, they all find a place.

The studio is now the centre of my photographs. When I decide I want to make a picture, I find somebody who wants to work with me, someone I know I like or want to work with, or simply whoever's available. We go to the studio and there we start. The ideas come sometimes from them, sometimes from me, it doesn't matter. The one with my son, Lucas, and the dog, Tarso, is a rare one taken without active cooperation: they didn't have too much to say on the matter. My models often lose their heads in my work – lose them to animals. Sometimes the animals are also fragmented or disappear altogether in the process. The blowfish I was brought as a present, already dead. I photographed it with the man, then hung it in a tree until it got eaten and not even the skin was left. This photograph *is* the blowfish.

The birds, the geese, get used alive. But you can see from the way they're held that the models know how to handle them. Manuel decided to squeeze the baby birds up to his eyes, tiny ones who fell out of their nest. He rescued them and held them so delicately, so tenderly, while I photographed him, then put them back. The other picture with the covered eyes was requested by this friend of mine who's dying of AIDS, who requested an epitaph. Putting bronze – like coins – on the eyes of the dead is a common custom, so maybe I acted instinctively when he asked me to choose something to hold and I gave him one of my father's sculptures. The man cradling the little Christ: I liked the expression on his face and his hands.

Man with Christ
1991

In making a selection of my photographs, we have to end with these giant seafish we call *cavala* [a kind of mackerel]. I like the story of this picture. It came from a photograph [my son] Christian did of a fisherman. It was good but it still seemed to me there was something missing in it. So I decided to make one of my own, to try and show him what was the magic ingredient. At that time there was a *pedreiro* [stonemason] working on our house, and when I told him *Manuel, vamos a fazer umas fotos do peixe* [Manuel, let's take some fish pictures], you know what? He was very pleased with the result and when I asked him about it, he said 'oh well, I was a fisherman for many years before becoming a *pedreiro*'. We hear a lot about how the camera always lies. But to me, in an unexpected sort of way, it always arrives at the truth. That's the kind of photography I deal with.

Interviews made at Rio Vermelho, Salvador, in June 1993 and February 1994

Lord of the head
1988

Vodun figure
1988

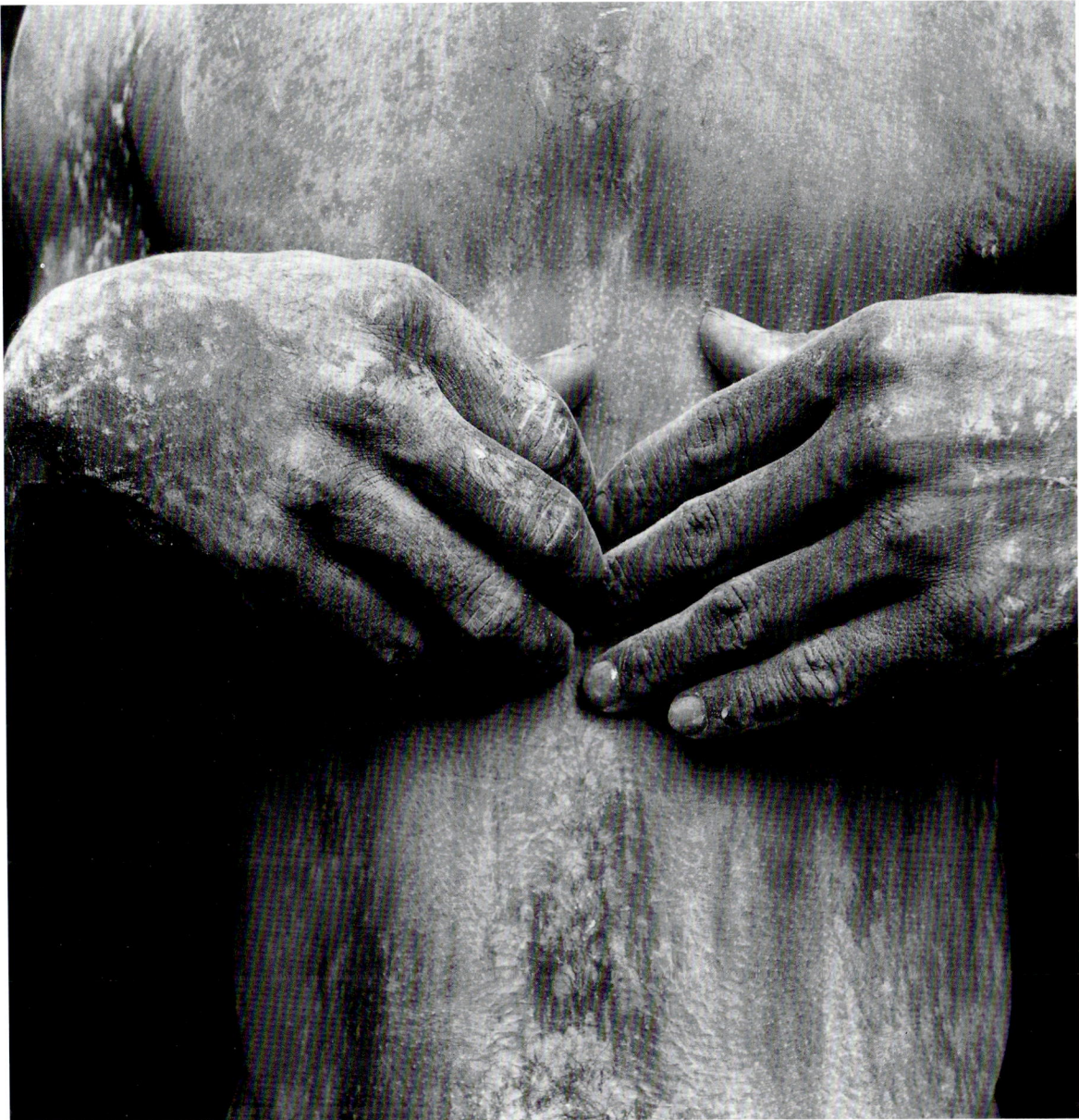

Black torso in whitewash
1988

Untitled

Sacrifice
1989

Vodun child
1989

Mask
1989

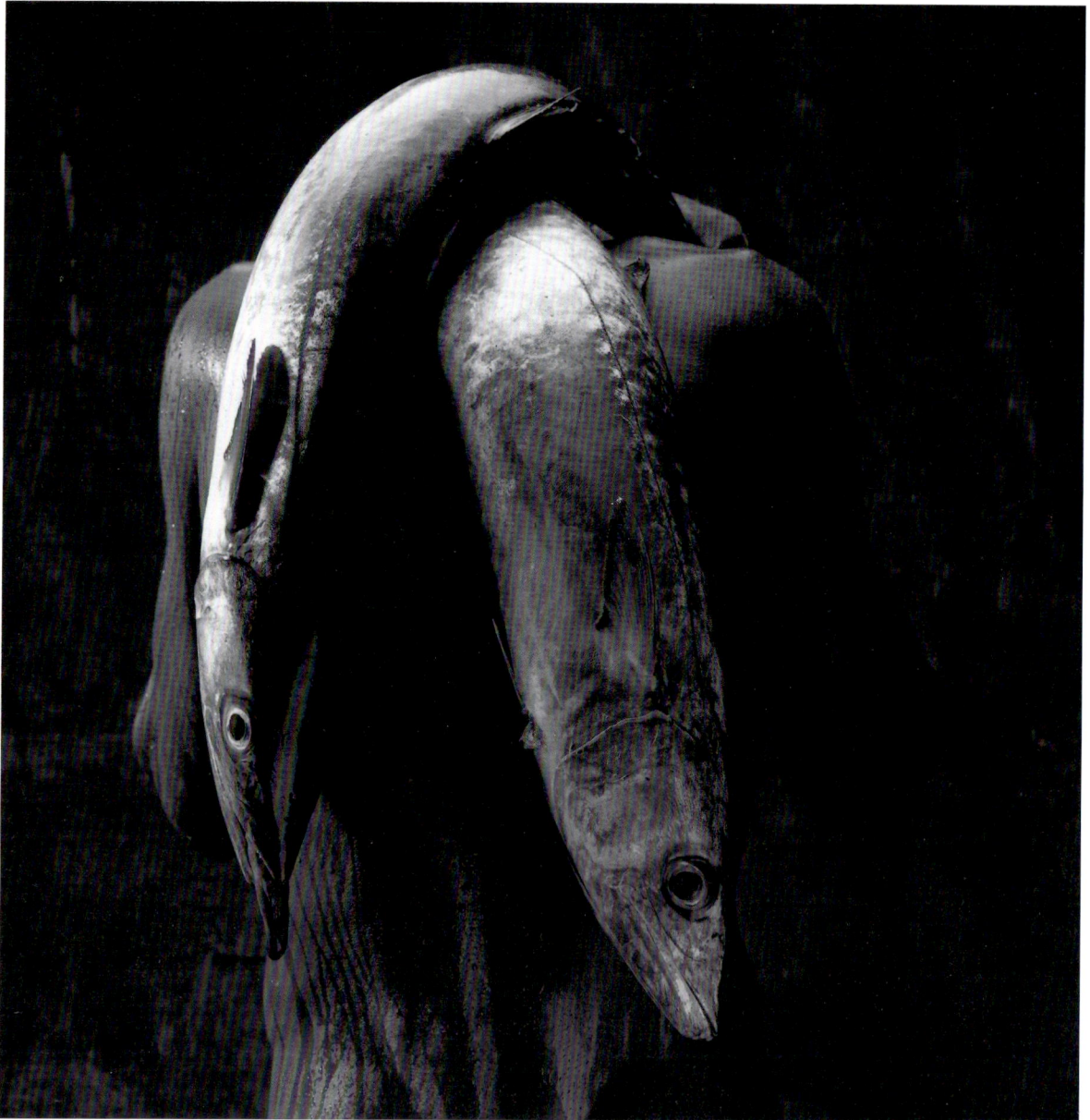

Man with two fishes
1992

Anna Mariani

Camaiura
indians

Making the fire
to glaze the
pots

We were talking about photographers as 'authors' or 'artists', and I was saying how I'd really rather talk about the work. I always remember an expression from my youth which said 'my work is my celebration', like a priest 'celebrating' the Mass. And that's the way it feels to me: my work is a celebration of nature and of light – sunlight, twilight, dawn and dusk. Every day I try to catch the sunrise, perhaps the most beautiful sight on earth, one that shouldn't be missed. In photographic terms, that's the celebration of my work, my office. For me, to describe myself as an 'author' is over the top. But to talk of that task of celebration is already a lot, is quite enough.

I only take photographs of Brazil, and of northeast Brazil. I've tried to photograph here where I now live in São Paulo, because I love the vitality of the city, its explosive and disorganised enormity. As a metropolis it fascinates me, yet I'm quite incapable of capturing that fascination in my images. Since others succeed where I've failed, there's no point in pushing it. We live in times so saturated with images that one can feel a sense of guilt simply for adding to them. And so I return to the things that seem to me eternal, to do with the light and the land,

a different atmosphere that perhaps I'm capable of relaying.

It's a way of perceiving the world. For me that crimson frieze on the horizon at sunset, that's special to the *sertão*, in the Brazilian interior. It's a moment when one assumes the day is done, and then this light suddenly appears: precise, particular, nearly violent in its intensity. And silent. Silence is so important, I pursue it even in my series on the [house] façades, which I decided to arrange in this quiet way, to deliberately render them without impact. Where the shutters and doors weren't closed I asked the residents to seal them, I wanted that sense of the heat and the silence, although I wondered if that would make them unbearably boring. At least that's what everyone told me, and I had to go against them, but only because I wanted to remain true to my own way of seeing.

Of course there's another side to Bahia that we all know. It shows us [the capital] Salvador as a city in perpetual samba. That's true too. Salvador is an African city, it moves to the rhythm of the samba, everyone there seems to know how to move: just watch them dance! I always wonder if it's possible to arrive at the goals of material 'progress' amid so much sheer physi-

Glazing the pots

cal energy. Our country has paid a high price for so-called civilisation, for adopting capitalist goals. In Bahia, people still have an elemental energy, there aren't the same assumed commercial aims, the same work ethic. That's a fact of life, not good nor bad, only inexorable.

In my early work I looked at just how ancient – or 'primitive' – people's working conditions can be. I did several series on women's work, the first one on those who make terracotta pots. They glaze them in an immense open fire, horrifically hot in the heat of the day, using long branches to turn them as they glaze. They take so much trouble to create, decorate and bake their pots – and they're so fragile, so easy to break, sometimes just as they're being raked from the fire. The other irony is that the pots are for water, of which there's a terrible scarcity. Sometimes the women walk for miles to carry it back on their heads: it's an African scene. Sometimes I'm not sure how I can incorporate that sensation of watching a different way of moving, of being, in order to celebrate it, understanding a little bit more about Africa as I watch.

That series I called a *queima de acha* (after the wood fires they burn) and decided to go onto a related one, where the women make manioc flour. I'd never consciously decided on taking women's work as a theme, but I agree with the Argentine writer Ernesto Sábato when he says: 'It's not us who select our theme; the theme chooses us'. Whenever I'm asked 'Why do you decide to do this ... or that?' I don't know why, exactly. So Sábato's conclusion seems subtle and sympathetic.

Another writer whose work I like very much, and who helped set me on my way is Ariano Suassuna. He telephoned me out of the blue one day, and expressed a common interest in the landscapes of the northeast. Specifically the fact that they still so closely resemble those painted by Frans Post, a Dutch painter who came out to Brazil with Maurice of Nassau in the seventeenth century. Post returned to the Netherlands with a mass of sketches to paint from; several of his works ended up in the Louvre, others in London's National Gallery and, of course, in the Rijksmuseum in Amsterdam. Suassuna had the idea of creating a group show with a graphic artist, a watercolourist and a photographer, who would each give their version of Post's universe. At first I found the idea pretentious, but agreed to join in out of respect for Suassuna. I also asked to be allowed to leave the coastline that Post hugged and go into the interior.

Today the skies are still as wide, and it's possible to view them with great pools of shadow in the foreground and lines of light behind, according to Post. For me his look became a school of vision and involved learning to predict when clouds would overcast the foreground, revealing a backlit landscape. Every image became tinted by that relationship of light and shadow, skies tinged with Post's tonalities. Things I'd never previously considered. The exhibition tour retraced Frans Post's travels, to Pernambuco and Olinda, through 1991, before coming to São Paulo. Here it was staged for the first International Photography Month held in Latin America in May 1993.

It was in working on this that I really came to know the region up in Pernambuco, the sugarcane zone where I fell in love with the semi-desert, with thousands of flowers amid the aridity, growing close to the ground, burgeoning after the sudden rainfalls. The only 'artist' in all this was undoubtedly Frans Post, while I was there as a photographer, learning from his vision of our world. In any case, I think artistry is always in the eye of the other. It's like you never quite believe someone who keeps telling you how truthful they are. It's an opinion that carries a lot more clout when expressed by others.

Grinding the manioc flour

So here we are, back with my work, my 'office of celebration'. I guess it began by chance, at an airport back in 1968 when a cousin, who was seeing me off on holiday, was horrified that I didn't have a camera to take snapshots. I didn't even want a camera but when I reached Greece the light, like they all say, so captivated me that I picked up the camera he'd bought me. It coincided with reading a biography of Paul Klee which described his going to Africa for the first time. He was a professional musician at that time although he'd already started painting, and as soon as he encountered the light there he announced 'I'm a painter'. Not 'I'm an *auteur*' or even 'an *artiste*'. And I felt something similar in Greece, again in a very arid landscape which resembled the northeast I know so well, and I was caught be the light. And so I, in my turn, of course tried to catch the light, that intangible fading between the hours…

Those early photographs are dreadful, but they show the same preoccupation with tone, colour and a light seeking to be both tender and subtle. I can line up my most recent prints alongside them and see the resemblance, since the same things still interest me. I've never been so concerned with form, I don't even know if I could undertake things in a formal manner. That perhaps has to do with the fact that it was then, in the 1960s, I had to abandon my career as a dancer, and dance – to me – is similar to drawing. They are both about cadence, about movement. I was classically trained, had five children, but never gave up dancing until I had polio, which damaged my spine. That was when I took up photography, an 18-month course here in São Paulo. It was where I also came to know [the English photographer and tutor] Maureen Bisilliat, who invited me to collaborate in a group show that included Cristiano Máscaro. I contributed an early series on women workers, those working with sisal to make brooms. In 1970, it was the women making manioc flour. And then, at the Museum of Modern Art, the women glazing their ceramic pots. That won the Museum prize.

Making sisal brooms

A colleague, Gabriel Zellmeister also helped edit the exhibition of landscapes juxtaposed with façades. We started with over 2000 slides laid out on 30 light-boxes at the photography school and worked down from there. Maureen Bisilliat went round them all saying: 'But you haven't selected this one, or that one. You always eliminate the best'. She couldn't see why, but it's because the series is always of more significance than the individual image. And you make a fresh selection according to whether it's for a book or a gallery and the scope you're given.

What you exclude depends on what you include in the sequence, not on how a single shot stands alone.

And the others, those who thought that there was nothing more boring than 60 façades of traditional houses in the *sertão*, seem to have come round. I think the whole media is so anti-boredom it desensitises us to the fact that there are lots of ways of being – even of arranging 55 images, all of the same size and subject in a single book. My rhythm happens to go with the pages, to be anti-video clip. It's the way I am, I can't do otherwise, it simply wouldn't be worth the attempt to try. And so I arranged my sequences for the 1987 Biennale here in São Paulo, and a parallel show travelled to Europe. For New York's PS1 Gallery I combined the façades in diptychs with images from the *caatinga*, the semi-arid zone. I first of all attempted to combine the landscapes in creating all the seasons in a 24-hour timespan. The Biennale always takes place in a huge mall, and I had three rooms in which to create dawn, noon and dusk, like the seasons of the year.

In the book I did it differently, going from the simplest to the more complex designs. Meaning that the first picture is of a white house with white doors and shutters, and the colours are introduced gradually. In the Biennale there were mini spotlights I could use to create what

I call the 'tangential shadows' cast at either end of the day, and strip lighting to reproduce the sun at midday. Between the two twilights, in which only the images were illuminated, came a whitened room, apparently filled with a noonday sun. Jean Baudrillard [who wrote the afterword to the French edition] called it a 'geometric frieze from a subequatorial Palace of Minos'. It seemed to be well-received by others too: over 250,000 visited the Biennale.

As a result I received three further invitations for the Staatlicher Kunsthalle in Berlin; the Pompidou Centre in Paris; and the Finnish Museum of Architecture. All those exhibitions took place, along with another in London – one of those occasions you never quite fathom. Someone took a catalogue of my work into the Serpentine Gallery, they decided they wanted it, persuaded me to get involved, and included a fresh run alongside an exhibition of paintings. The press picked up on the façades, and it merited a write-up in the Saturday *Independent* and *Time Out*.

And now I'm building a series of diptychs to bring to London, a new edit of fresh images. And that work really goes back sixteen years, when I first started travelling in the region, photographing in black and white and processing in my kitchen while the children were at school. I became so addicted that I began to see in black and white, worse still seeing in negative, as I was beginning to learn to work directly onto the negs. When I work, it's a living – a lived – obses-

Sorting the sisal for brooms

sion. I thought at first I was taking architectural shots because I was working alongside an architect, but then I found I was simply working in the only way I know how.

Which means that, along with every photographer from the 'Third World', I get criticised because my work isn't directly 'social', even documentary. Well, it fits what I see as reality: for example, eleven solid years' work celebrating the fact that people out in the *sertão* have, for hundreds of years, found the money – out of nowhere! – to do what they're not assumed to be capable of, painting beautiful dwellings. No commercial enterprise is remotely interested in those people without money to spare or to spend. But I guess you somehow find the money for what is most important to you. Even paint. And the people there paint their houses this crazy way, a mixture of early Dutch architecture – as Post shows – with vivid colour and a complete lack of symmetry. Supposedly it's the only asymmetric folk architecture, and I didn't even notice, I was so taken with it. My images provoked a political scenario I'd never intended, at least among the critics, about how the poorest of the poor discover their capacity to organise themselves in the cause of beauty.

Then there was the exhibition of my work on the semi-arid region, to coincide with the international Ecology Conference in Rio in 1992. All anyone wanted to hear about there was the Amazon, the Amazon, not the semi-arid zones. And yet this is a vast and important region, and

I didn't want the world to continue ignoring its existence… I really believe, along with [the film-maker] Glauber Rocha, that it's an area capable of enormous changes: one minute you can say it's the apotheosis of white light, it looks so dry and bleached, and the next it's a brilliant green.

On the one hand I started there because I wanted to rediscover my own roots, those of my family who immigrated from Italy around 1760 and travelled down the São Fransisco river. On the other, I owe an immense debt to [the author] Euclides da Cunha. I take a copy of *Os Sertões* (Rebellion in the Backlands) each time I travel there, and the Portuguese edition of my book ends with an excerpt from it. The *sertão* series has been called an illustrated homage, and when I read him I feel drunk with inspiration! I'm not the only one: there are also a couple of North American film-makers out there looking to make a movie about a one-eyed bandit who used to roam there, Lampiaò, and his girl-friend Maria Bonita, about whom the folk song was written. We all share the same passion for this strange semi-arid place, bare of so much, including tourists. The full river … the full moon … you feel it all belongs to you. Magical.

For me that goes back to my sense of place, of origin and belonging. I only photograph when I see something I know, there's an established familiarity. A few years ago I was in southern Morocco, I remarked on certain similarities in the way they paint their houses, their shutters. I took some photographs that weren't bad, but dare say the Moroccans might have done them better. Of course that's the antithesis of a western attitude. Look at the Magnum agency, sending photographers around the world to make their stamp on it. There are plenty of other styles of working, some as successful as Cartier-Bresson's book on India. That's their talent, it's not mine. I need to work more slowly, to find the time to achieve something I want to show, that might give the viewer pleasure.

People always ask me if I've an oriental way of working and I sometimes amuse myself by answering that I'm a Taoist. Because I've studied Taoism, without going into it too deeply but enough to know that we shouldn't be discussing oriental philosophy but oriental practices. It's the same whether we are discussing Tao or Zen. *The Art of the Zen Archer* is a book by E Herrigel, a German philosopher from Heidelberg who taught Kantian philosophy at a Japanese university for many years. He was trying to learn Tai Ch'i and the art of the archer. Each time he asked his teacher: 'But how, but how? Please explain it to me' his teacher would never explain, but simply practiced and told him to practice.

I'm not too keen on explanations either. I believe that you can arrive through practice rather than theory. So I've worked hard at Tai Ch'i Chuan every day for the last nine years, and I don't stop to score points for achievement, though every day brings its own. To me, photography is exactly the same. Attention and practice are the only ways to achievement. Paying attention teaches you to see the less visible aspects of things, sharpens your way of looking. It's about realisation, disclosing and developing something that was always there, you've seen but perhaps you've never really viewed before.

You can see I'm no great intellectual! I've accumulated almost no books of photography theory. All I know is that I keep working at it. Yet there seems to be no escape from philosophy. When Jean Baudrillard saw my façades at the Biennale and wanted to meet me, to write an afterword for the French edition to coincide with my exhibition at the Beaubourg, I didn't even know who he was. But I invited him down to the country for Sunday lunch, there were plenty of other people there, and he could stay quietly abstracted in his corner. Perhaps the lack of threat or pressure allowed him to figure out what to write for himself.

I'm hard put even to give you any photographic influences: I love the work of [the Mexican photographer, Alvarez] Bravo, and of the North American Richard Misrath, of Marc Riboud. But I don't belong to any photographic coterie, I'm not on any circuit. The biggest influence, if you insist, would probably be Maureen [Bisilliat] saying: 'Never start shooting in broad daylight, always at twilight'. That's what teaches you about colour, what has helped me to find *my* colour, a colour that is almost colourless. The division of the back- and foreground I learnt from Frans Post.

None of that is at the front of my mind when I'm out taking photographs. Then there's no decision, just an overwhelming sense of reality, the impression that in my work I realise who I am. I'm in love with that light, that region. That's all.

Interviews in São Paulo, June 1993, and London, December 1993

Brazilian cowboy

Miguel Rio Branco

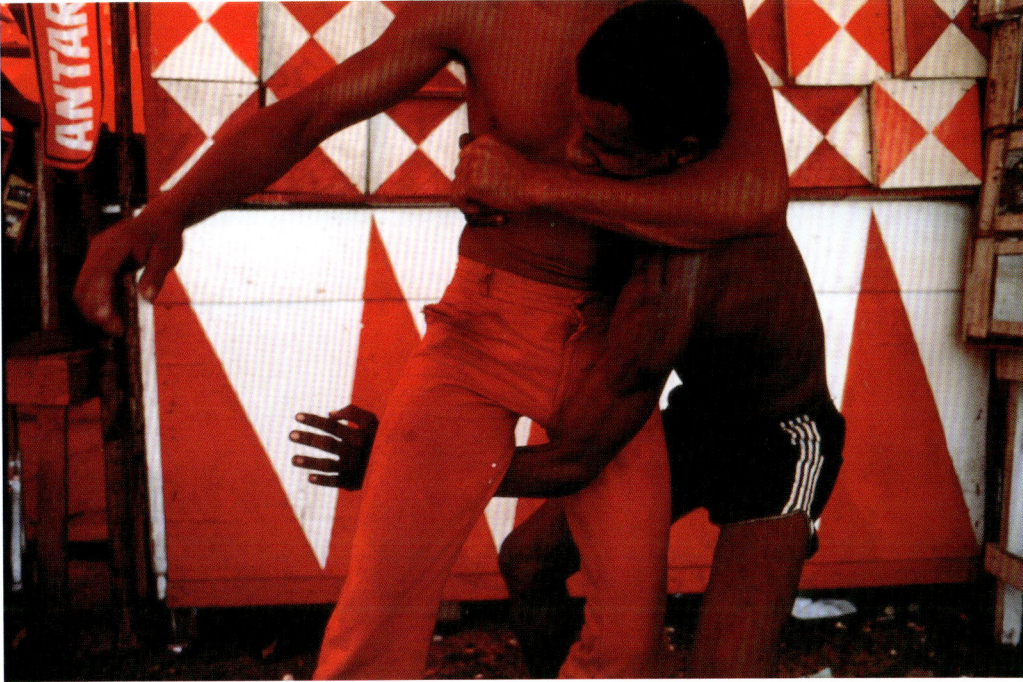

My interest in photography began when I was still at school, through a friend who had a beautiful camera. I was studying in Switzerland at the time. Although I was interested in geology, I already knew that my main subjects were painting and drawing. The photographs I took were almost all touristic. The camera – one of the very first twin-lens Reflex ones, a beautiful thing – was of considerably more interest than the possibility of making photography itself the tool.

It was in Switzerland, in 1964, that I had my first exhibition – of paintings, not photos. Then my family moved to New York where I continued my studies, just painting for myself and including photographs in the collages as well as using them as reference points. Still really playing with the camera. A lot of pictures of objects, architecture, few people, but already a strong focus on basic textures and colours. My photography is really not all that colourful, although once in a while reds or blues come up, and the same goes for the paintings: for both I always choose a restricted palette. If you look at my paintings from New York in 1966, you can already find the basis of the same attitude I have today, to colour in my work.

Of course my work uses colour, and I always get told how 'very Brazilian' it is. Yet most of it is really monochromatic variations, not primary colours. There's nothing flash or snappy in my work! I work with available light, and my range relates more to painting than to photography. For me photography remains something very personal, that has to do with you and your position in the world. It becomes possible to say things through your work that others can understand, wherever they come from. The individual story behind the image doesn't matter, it's not a question of exhuming its origins.

I had one more painting exhibition, in 1967, before leaving New York, then showed at the São Paulo Biennale in 1967. Then I entered the School of Industrial Design in Rio, partly because I felt I needed to do something more understandable. That's when you begin to concentrate on photography – and of course fall into the trap it sets for you. I fell into the trap through my own ignorance: I just had the usual assumptions about the medium. I hadn't read any books, apart from Bill Brandt. I think what I liked most in him was his anguished climate, the dark skies and so forth. He showed that you could convey an inner climate within a supposedly representational image, although this wasn't a lesson I learnt right away. It was a long time, in fact, before I properly understood, and of course things varied in the course of Brandt's career. It was his early pictures of coalminers which, although they had no direct influence on what I photographed, taught me about texture and mood.

In 1970 I went back to New York, having made my first – important – contact with Bahia. It was to work in a movie with the film director Arnaldo Jaboa, on the island of Itaparica, and it gave me the opportunity to work with Alfonso Beato, the director of photography. He already liked what I was doing, but it gave me the chance to work in two formats, making stills and slide shows in black and white and colour, staying three months on the island since we didn't have the facilities there to keep checking on the rushes. That was where I first really got to work in colour, the film had a strong contact with colour, it was a period film set in the 1500s that served as a metaphor for Brazil. A lot of the people working on it were *baianos* and the whole region made a deep impression on me.

Anyway, back to New York until 1972. Another world, an American story in which I was shooting mainly black and white, street shots of the East Side, the Bowery. All stuff related to my daily life. I already had this thing about learning… I attended a School of Visual Arts for a month. Then I left, when I realised they were teaching me things I knew already. I'd be the first to say I was never really a good student, even at school. Only during the last year in Switzerland, when my painting began to be accepted

did *I* begin to feel accepted. But concerning the School of Visual Arts: I wanted to move up a year; they refused to let me; I left the School.

Perhaps necessarily, I came to believe that you learn more – visually – from keeping your eyes open and looking around. Just from being yourself, even if you're not yet fully conscious of who you might become. At that time I was painting figuratively, nothing like the abstract work I'm doing now. The desire to get to some basic essence that might be described as the meaning of life, that remains the same. And sometimes you surprise yourself with what you find in your own work. In my photographs it's there in the recent work on the boxing academy: the played-out old man with the tender eyes; the guy doing press-ups, a rapid movement that's impossible for the photographer to control; the boxer fighting partly behind the blue curtain. It's all a little more graphic than I'd anticipated.

Yet the series that have been of most recent interest to me are the most abstract, some so dark they're almost blacked out, one with just a snake showing. Very Baroque. Those, from Barcelona, contain more information for me than perhaps anything else I've done: almost the exact opposite to my work in Bahia. There, you can see the whore with the scarred back, you know her story. Or the two women laughing, playing on the bed together. I called one show that came from there *I won't take anything with me you can't repay me in Hell,* a slogan that was written on a wall in the prostitutes' area of Salvador. But I think the most interesting images, those that last, are not a direct representation of reality but something more subtle and introverted. In Barcelona I hardly shot any people on the streets when I went around, and the apparent solitude and sense of introversion suited me.

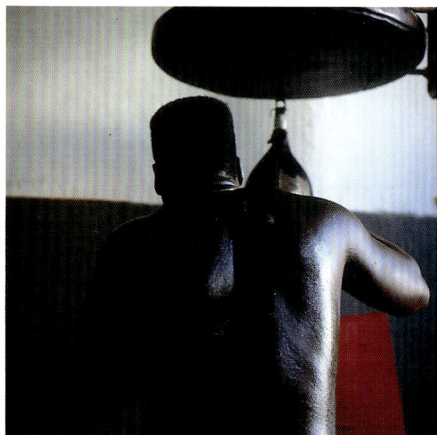

The more you publish, the more you see how little control you have over how the material gets used. A lot happens you feel misrepresents what you're doing, misleads the viewer. I have a very particular way of putting my pictures together: that's my main subject, the montage thing. I started twenty years ago with an exhibition that travelled from Rio to São Paulo then out of the country, huge rough sheets of paper collaged with pictures in varying arrangements. I already knew I didn't want to be trapped in one style, one way of showing pictures. And that came partly from my work in the movies, when you have to realise that the images have to work in relation to one another, so they create a poem, or together construct a statement.

You learn a standpoint that's between the real and the abstract, almost the epitome of whatever it is you need to convey – here it's the sensuality of the image, there it's an expression of pain. The body of work is very much to do with Bahia: I had completely different experiences in both Europe and the United States. It was a rite of passage for me. Here, prostitutes are commonly a boy's first sexual encounter. The first time I went into a whorehouse was there, in 1974. It was both very shocking and very attractive; you can learn a lot about a country in that way! For me too, it was important to learn something about that mixture of pleasure and pain there at its sharpest. If you know anything of the history of art, you know what a classic scenario that is.

When I first went into the Pelourinho area and met those models you see, there was both a type of intensity and a type of eternity in their expressions, their skin – the texture of skin is always fundamental to me. So many of them are scarred, some by their clients, some do it themselves. The one there has small cuts made with a razor right the way up her leg. She says the cuts represent the number of men she has loved. The one with the really damaged leg, that's a medical condition, but it's also her thing, what's special about her. I photographed the series in 1979, sending the film back and forth to be developed in São Paulo, to give the women back their images. Not that they were so very interested; the pleasure/pain ratio is pretty unequally distributed between the clients/whores.

The whole thing was not undertaken as a photojournalistic essay but really as an essay in dealing with those fundamental issues of human life. It was also a coming to terms with power [relations]; I'd never come across any form of authority that to me seemed to work, that's why I was always such a rebellious student. And, seeing how politics are conducted in this country left me mistrustful of granting authority to one person over another... From when I was young, I was always reacting against what was around me, but I always got away with it, in a way, because I was also very funny. In a way that's the tension.

It's very hard to determine when something becomes exploitative, at what point one should stop taking pictures. You always try to stay on the right side of the barrier and can see that, when people start doing things out of self-promotion, to line their own pockets, then you know they've fallen foul. When I take photographs like these, that also have to do with the pain in someone's life, I agree with Flaubert: *Madame Bovary, c'est moi.* Of course all this work is subjective; in that sense it's about me. When it begins to work is when you're revealing yourself. Pain has no sex, it's not about a woman, someone I do or don't desire. It really doesn't matter if I find the woman attractive, the photograph of her is *my* work.

The women accepted my presence and I started giving them portraits, with little slide viewers. The film really didn't interest them too much, it was too expressionist, if you like, more about the human situation than just about them. Very few women *didn't* want to be photographed. People there anyway often tend to be more open; it's not like taking pictures here in Paris. I began to see that however traditional and good the reportage one could do, one needed to get beyond that. There was less discouragement in *not* seeing photography as a means to change the world. Photography of course is very limited: there are other means of expression, like painting, which remain much freer.

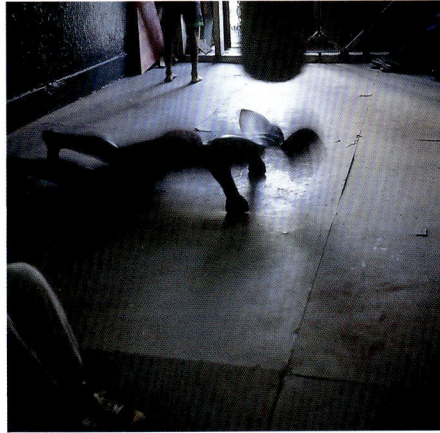

So the nature of my work is changing. I travel less, and I can take a sketch book as well as a camera where I go. I have a different – consistent – signature. There are so many solitary dogs in my pictures, witnesses like the photographer. I'm a bit of a dog myself. The best work I've ever done was on the reflections of a dog before dying, shown at the Arles Festival in 1991 as a slide show against an underground chapel wall. Obviously those aspects of life and death are there, in a relationship, human and animal, man and dog.

Some of the things – like that – I've done and assume no one else has done. But sometimes you find someone you admire, like I do Robert Frank, and discover that you've been working along remarkably similar lines for a long time. That identity, of identification, can recur throughout your working life as a photographer. Or, back at the 1983 Biennale in São Paulo, I made a five-screen installation in a dark room with the images running through five carousels, like shuffling a deck of cards. There was one indian boy who remained constant, standing against a pink wall, dialoguing with all the other images, mostly symbolic of this so-called modern society. And when I was preparing the show I came across an old copy of *Camera* magazine and found early pictures by Christer Stronhölm, a Swedish photographer, working with the same intentions as I.

But I wouldn't say that most of my influences are photographic. There's been more directly from painting, or from music. Music is always quite important, even to accompany my work. It depends on the mood, sometimes it's classical, sometimes just the human voice. A woman's voice. Women are always bound to be important: they're the basis of a positive aspect of human life. To accompany the five-screen installation with its multiple images there were different rhythms, and the speed of the images varied accordingly. It's something to do with the rhythm of life, woman at its source and decay – the dying dog if you like – at its end. Death is decomposition, another variation of nature. And we're all getting older…

Time is a basic given of life and no one knows what it is. It relates to everything, sometimes we live in past memories, sometimes in future projects. It changes all the time – and I'm using that work still without having reached a definition of it. Photography obviously captures the moment, in that sense freezes time, yet that doesn't endow it with any special significance to me. The fact that it's always looking back – the image you've just taken is already in the past – and that links it to a process moving towards death and decay matters more to me.

The first time I went out on the indian project was during their festival of the turtles, as you see them bringing them in on that great pole. So I persuaded the *National Geographic* to send me back and catch something more of their daily life. I'd been looking to return as a photographer for a long time, having been a cameraman on three movies to do with the indians. I was still out there really on a quest for a better society, one that had not been destroyed in the way ours is. *That* vain hope. One night the indians were doing their dance of the *arara*, around and around in a circle, to a single repetitious sound, rather like a cricket's. I took my tape recorder and began taping, as it seemed important to keep that sound with the indian images. Somehow, although I was working there with an anthropologist/writer, it was more important to get to a personal, even a poetic statement, not to just do another piece of anthropology.

The ideal assignment was like the one I had earlier in 1993, when the Banesto Foundation allowed me to do whatever it was I needed as a personal project in Barcelona. Everyone else selected is a traditional reportage photographer, but the only requirement was to produce a certain number of pictures, no strings. The music to accompany it is the opera you hear around you now, in this gallery. One of the favourite pictures is again of the dead bird beside the tiny egg. Back playing with ideas of life-cycles, death and time… again.

The other project I'm working on is the boxing academy at Lapa, in the former town centre of Rio. It's something I'm taking to a festival in Havana for May 1994 and is also on a retrospective theme. There's an old gym in a rundown area where there are a lot of prostitutes and transvestites working. The walls have these peeling cutouts reporting past fights and victories, and I'm arranging the show to have rolls of newsprint mounted with programmes, period portraits and magazine pages going back to the 1920s, with my own colour images mounted alongside them. It all gets laid out in crossed panels and the room fills with sound – all the nostalgia in the tunes and songs of fifty or more years ago. That also fits with another period in Havana's history, before the 1958 revolution, when it was a kind of rough joint, a crook's playground.

What's interesting about the boxing series is that it's not really about boxers. It's like having a map of humanity, all the precariousness and uncertainty of existence. There's a confrontation there, between them as fighters, them against the world – and of course with me, confronting them through the camera. Because the photographer's always present too: there's nothing objective about photography. You never get to tell the whole story. You can show something about the boxers or – another story I've been working on – the street children around the Candelaria [Church in Rio], but it's never the story of the country, never even the story you'd like to tell. And the press also have a real part to play, the way they present things. We have a virtual civil war in Rio, and the press refuses to acknowledge what's happening. They only see the boys being killed. It's not just Rio's problem, either, it connects to other countries, the way we're all economically linked.

The children don't go to school; the imported films on television are all about violence; their role models are Rambo or Supergun; their lives are on the streets. How are they going to get a living, how are they going to behave – like angels? They're not children in the sense they have a childhood, in the sense of being protected. In all these portraits of children you see the vulnerable need to be a child, it's obvious. At the same time they can kill you as they would a fly, it's been made so completely normal. And the television discussions lamenting it never at all outweigh the diet of violence on the screen the rest of the time. What I'd like to do is to return and follow these kids' stories in far more detail, take one in particular and let it unfold like a novel, tell the whole story. Like this one, the pregnant girl. It has to be a form of fatalism, at fifteen, to feel that life has to be proved to continue in that way, already having a baby.

I don't have the sensation of belonging to only one place. I could as well belong here in Paris or New York. Belonging is connected to images, to language, to history. Of course the indians in Brazil are more foreign to me than Europeans here, we belong to different countries. There was a time I was more photographically concerned with those 'other countries', took a lot of pictures of the *candomblé* [Afro-Brazilian religion] for example, and then it was all lost in a fire at my studio in São Paulo, in 1980. I lost many sets of negs and prints there; perhaps a lesson in not belonging, not becoming too attached to homes or possessions…

Bahia, for me, was about living in a house at the edge of the sea, near Itapoa. It lasted, on and off, for ten years to 1989 and it was there I returned to painting as my main interest. The pictures of the women there were done without there being any obvious relationship there, they look very natural, they behaved very sympathetically towards me. My role was more as a portraitist, the pictures appeared in *Aperture*, as photojournalism. I guess it changed my views of humanity a bit. It's a parable of survival in distress, you can apply it to anywhere you like in Brazil, even as a metaphor of the country as a whole, just like the street children. There's nothing easy about it at all.

Interviews in Paris, November 1993 and Rio de Janeiro, February 1994

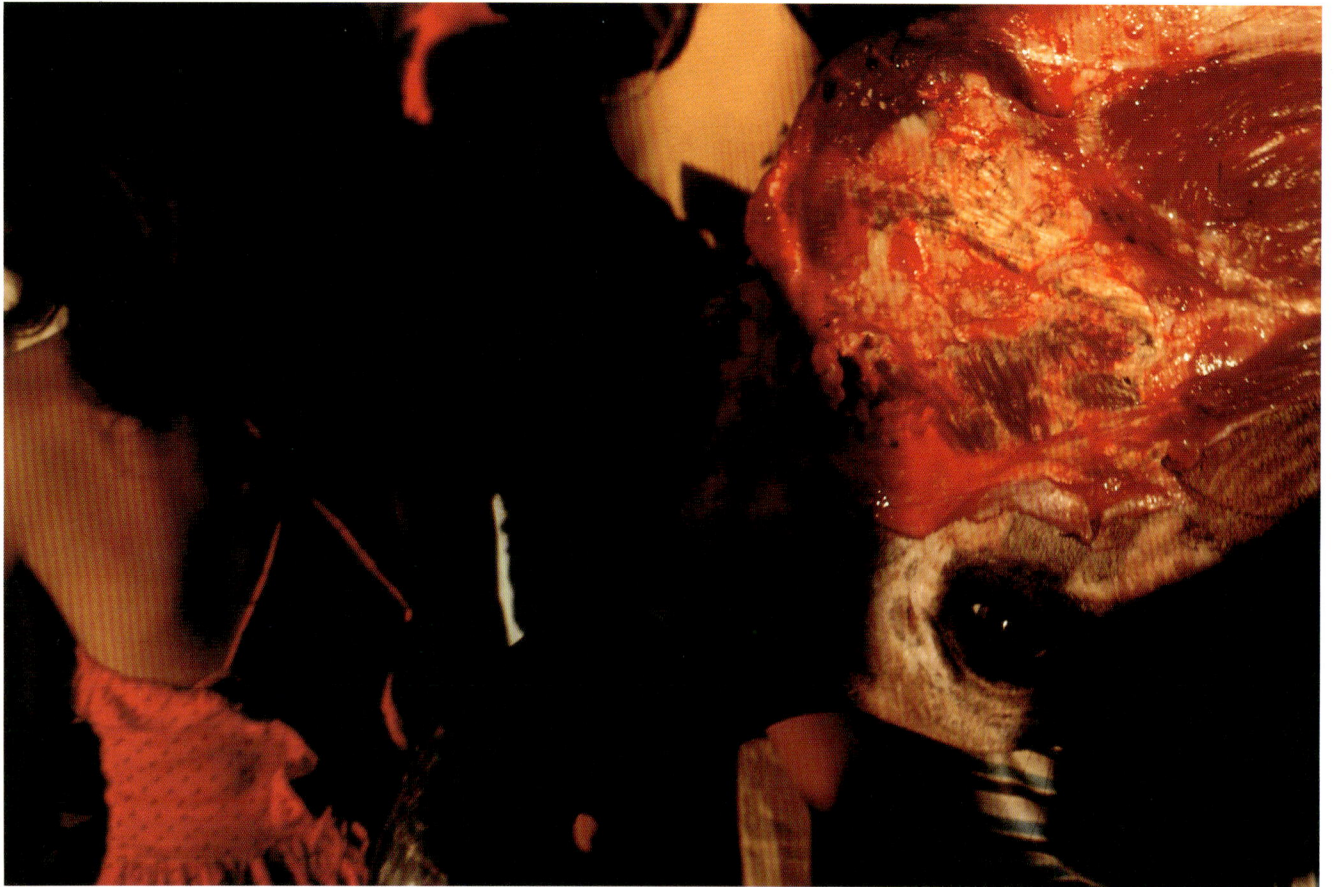

Luiz Figueiredo

Xica da Silva

Apparition

Brothel

Clown

L uiz Figueiredo, the Brazilian naïve painter, was born in 1944 in the town of Cuiabá, State of Mato Grosso, and is known as one of the most original and talented artists of this genre in Brazil. He paints, sculpts and designs colourful tapestries and wall hangings. His art is inspired by the popular culture, the traditions and the folklore of Brazil which he views and depicts with candid and humorous spontaneity. His love of street festivals, both sacred and profane, of opera, theatre and carnival gives him themes to explore in his vividly coloured canvases. He uses the images of the people he meets in the exotic night world of cities such as Salvador and Rio de Janeiro. The prostitutes, the transvestites, the sailors and the performers can all be seen theatrically portrayed in his paintings. Luiz Figueiredo is a mature artist who manages to retain a naïve freshness and 'joie de vivre' in all his work.

With his masterful use of papier mâché he creates sculptures of mermaids, gods and goddesses of the Afro-Brazilian rituals, dancers, clowns, horses and saints, that are an incredible fusion of the so-called Brazilian baroque with expressionism. He combines symbolism and folklore to create a colourful rich world of his own. Luiz's 'Blue Orixá' papier mâché sculptures of a God has been used as the symbol of the Festival of Bahia organised by Brazilian Contemporary Arts in London in May 1994 and appears on all the publicity material, an eye-catching and vital figure.

Luiz Carlos Figueiredo grew up in the small town of Conservatoria in the interior of the State of Rio de Janeiro. He began to paint and work with papier mâché in 1961 inspired by the scenes of his childhood. In 1965 he moved to Belo Hor-

Circus girl on horseback

izonte in Minas Gerais where he ran a bar and co-founded an art studio for children. Some of his vibrant use of colour and his world of make-believe stem from this period. From Belo Horizonte Luiz moved to Rio de Janeiro and then to Europe. He lived in Paris and then in Rotterdam where he still works for part of the year. He has exhibited in France, Holland, Germany, Spain, Belgium, Réunion, Argentina, Brazil and in 1993, for the first time, in London.

He has works in many private collections and is especially admired in France where one of the great critics of naïve art, Anatole Jacovsky of the International Museum of Naïve Art in Nice was inspired to write the following poem:

Par dessus les toits	*Above the roofs*
Par dessus les clochers	*Above the bellfries*
Par dessus la Seine	*Above the Seine*

Que voguent les Yamanjas	*Let the Yemanjás –*
Autrement dit les sirènes	
	Otherwise known as mermaids
De Luiz Carlos Figueiredo	
	Of Luiz Carlos Figueiredo – float

Luiz has always had a special feeling for the gods and goddesses of the Afro-Brazilian religions. As an adolescent he spent much time in Salvador in Bahia, often staying in the 'House of the Seven Dead' in the old Pelourinho area of the city. 'I was fascinated by the rituals of *candomblé* and the mysticism of the black population of Bahia. Many of my papier mâché sculptures are based on the colourful gods and goddesses of *candomblé* and my paintings show scenes of Umbanda rituals often including figures in their authentic costumes.'

Luiz Figueiredo now divides his year between

Yemanjá

Red Orixá

Nossa Senhora
de Concecão

his flat in Ipanema in Rio de Janeiro and his studio in Rotterdam. During the months of the Brazilian summer and carnival he is in Rio. He spends time with his many friends, goes to the beach, gives parties and renews his artistic inspiration in the exotic and theatrical night life of the city. He is the most generous of hosts and nothing is too much trouble for this kind-hearted man. Be it creating an amazing make up for a transvestite in a street carnival parade or organising an exotic fancy dress party for visiting friends, Luiz is always willing and ready to give his time. He is as warm and colourful as his paintings and is dearly loved by his friends.

His creativity in all fields is amazing. He will design pieces of colourful jewellery for the opening of an exhibition or fabricate a carnival costume from a few scraps of material and some feathers. To arrive at one of his parties unadorned is not a disaster! Within minutes you find yourself dressed as a clown, a bride, a pimp, made up as a cat or a drag queen and can merge unnoticed with as extraordinarily diverse a group of people as you would only expect to find on the set of a Fellini film! Luiz would love to use this talent for costume to one day be the designer for the parade of a Samba School. 'My dream would be to have the chance to create a whole fantasy world of floats and glorious costumes for one of the Schools of Samba. I would not need an enormous sum of money, just willing helpers and my imagination.'

Carnival Queen

As summer in Brazil comes to an end Luiz moves to Europe and his studio in the house of Pete Sluikerman in Rotterdam. It was while working there in Holland that the Dutch film maker Alex Boon came in contact with Luiz's work. Delighted by his colourful character and enchanted by his painting Alex Boon chose Luiz as one of the artists for a documentary film he was making on Dutch and foreign naïve painters. The film 'Adults in Wonderland' includes 30 minutes of Luiz working and playing in Brazil, very much the highlight of a delightful collection of filmed portraits of naïve artists.

In Holland Luiz likes to work at his painting and sculpture for several hours a day. 'Here in Rotterdam I can concentrate and work quietly without interruption', and he produces a large proportion of his work in this more peaceful environment.

Luiz Figueiredo is a personality; an artist who breaks conventions but does so in an enchanting and good-natured way. His baroque Madonnas could double as Carnival Queens, his transvestites as socialites from Rio. He has been praised by critics the world over as a candid, witty and spontaneous artist. He paints the world as seen through mischievously humorous eyes; he is recognised as one of the foremost naïve artists of his country and has been called the 'avant garde' naïve painter of Brazil.

Mairin Broughton

Portugal

Baiano Party

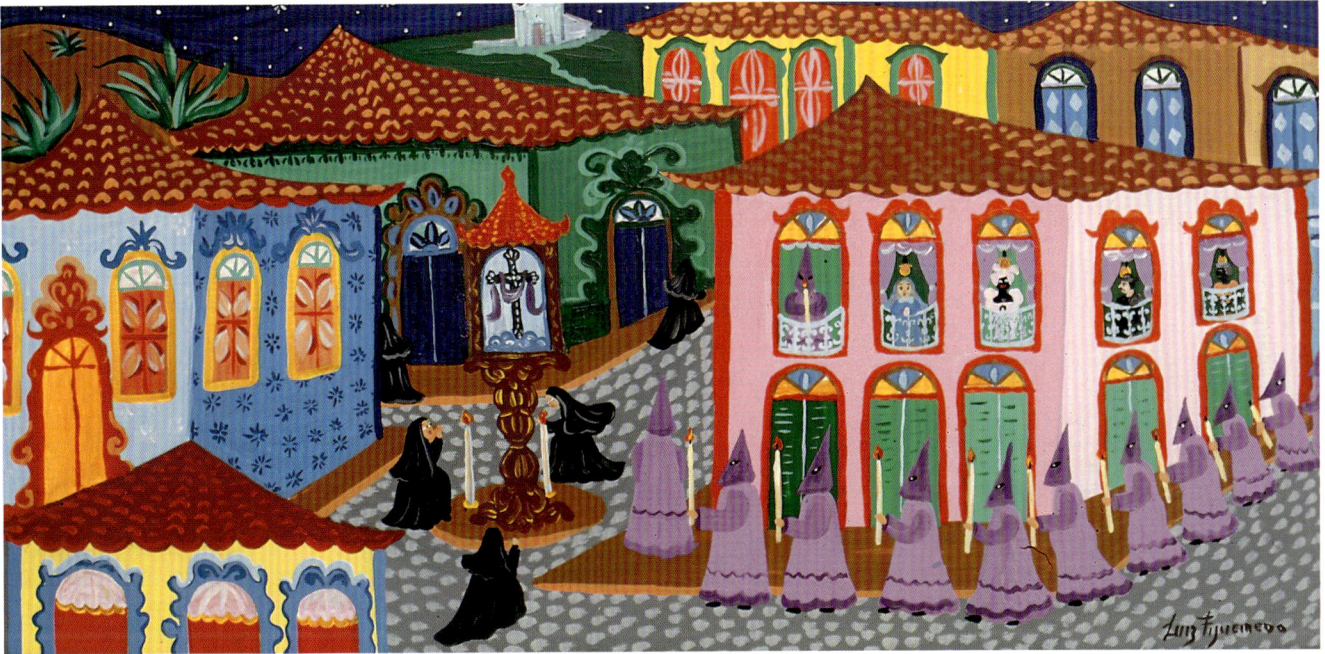

Pelourinho

Baiana

Postscript

It is with the greatest pleasure that I have chosen to introduce my friend Luiz Figueiredo, a very talented Brazilian artist whom I came to appreciate while I was Ambassador in Brazil and for whom I organised an exhibition in the French Embassy in Brazil.

Luiz Figueiredo is both a 'naïve' painter and a sculptor and such is his success in both disciplines that it is hard to say on which he excels most.

As an amateur of naïve paintings, I was charmed from the start by the virtuosity and spontaneity conveyed by his works in which vitality is constantly interlaced with humour.

However the experience and originality of his pallet are not limited to his paintings alone, they are also present in his papier mâché sculptures whose whimsical, sometimes uncanny characters bring to life a world of baroque poetic frenzy which is truly his own.

The collection presented here invites us, thanks to the artist's genius and to our great delight, to enter this enchanted world in which reality is totally transfigured.

Let me add that Luiz Figueiredo is also a man whose talent is matched by great tenderness and personal charm.

Bernard Dorin

French Ambassador to the United Kingdom

Carybé

Xangó, god of
fire and thunder

This visual record was begun forty-three years ago, in 1950, thanks to Rubem Braga, who introduced me to Anisio Teixeira, who introduced me to Governor Otávio Mangabeira, who engaged me to paint the portrait of Bahia.

That was how it started.

When I came to live here in 1950, something was happening that only takes place occasionally in this world. Happenings such as that in 1450 with the flowering of the Italian Renaissance. Followed by … the slide into obscurity. Or again, much later, the School of Paris. Another group of artists who gathered together – again the Italians, Hungarians, and above all Spaniards and just a few French artists, despite being called the 'Paris' School. So to 1950, and here, in its own tiny way, Bahia welcomed Hansen from Hamburg, myself from Buenos Aires, Jenner from Sergipe, while from São Paulo came a huge influx of people, Mario Cravo, himself a *baiano*, and Carlos Vascos returned from the United

A celebration to honour Oxún Miwá at
Mother Senhora's Opô Afonjá temple

Exorcism of the messenger Exú for Oxún,
at the Old Plantation

States and so there was a gathering, a flowering of new architecture, new sculpture and a whole new artistic movement.

That was how it started.

But – there is always a but – the taste of Bahia had been maturing in me like wine for twelve years, since our first encounter in 1938. That first encounter is what I first think of if you say 'Bahia' to me. I arrived by sea, under the impression that Bahia itself had waylaid the boat; that it was Bahia accompanying and mooring alongside us and not the other way around. At anchor and at home I descended into a magical kingdom. The character of the *baianos*, their music, the smells of local flowers and food, *acarajé* and pineapple. That year I was permanently ensnared by its light, its land and its sea. Even while I become increasingly infuriated at the construction-fever that creates so much noise and dust and unwanted buildings devouring the countryside. Even the sea is polluted but at least it remains the sea. What keeps me here is this magic which prevents me from entirely knowing what keeps me here.

Two great women of Oxún are the godmothers of this work: Nancy, with her support and encouragement, and the late Maria Bibiana do Espírito Santo, Mother Senhora, who welcomed us with great kindness and wisdom.

Yes indeed, it all began with great tramcar journeys to Cabula, Rio Vermelho, Liberdade, Bom Gosto, Federacão … journeys that were living audiovisual shows of windows, back yards, wells or ditches of red clay where life went on under the sun or by the light of the kerosene lamps and the moon. The sky was decorated with kites by day and fireworks by night, announcing the arrival of the *Orixás*.

Oxún, goddess of beauty and the River Oxún

Travelling on the Lower Rio Vermelho Line, in the last tramcar, the lovers' tramcar, you could overhear the hymns to Ogun and Yemanjá sung in the beautiful, powerful voice of Luis da Muriçoca, then a tram driver for the electricity company. Blend with that the rhythm of Cotinha de Oxumarê's drums and the discreet sound of the Adja of Aunt Massi, at the top of the steps leading to Casa Branca. In São Gonçalo, herds of cows passed through Retiro Park and the music of sacred hymns counterpointed the lowing of cattle and the songs of cowherds, filling the hollow of the night so that Oxossi could dance.

So you understand how I feel a *baiano* here – though if I return to Buenos Aires, I feel a *porteño* there, a *salteño*, if I travel to Salta. Since my father was Italian and I spent eight years of my childhood in northern Italy, I could pass there too, Spain, Portugal, England are all possible … Whereas I could never be a Pole or a German or a Hungarian. So I'm not quite a chameleon and

I belong to the culture of the *Orixás*. That is something for which I experience no fear, only respect.

This work is intended simply as an honest and precise record of the life of *candomblé*. The watercolours date from 1950 to 1993, showing festivals and vestments, the symbols and ceremonies I have witnessed in this prodigious world brought over with the slaves and deposited in the depths of Bahia's soul.

This is a world lovingly cared for by its adherents; a world of modest, human gods who still find themselves confronting the most terrible and voracious gods of modern times: progress, technology and science.

From Carybé's introduction to *Candomblé* [1993], and an interview in Bahia [1994]

Obá, goddess of the River Obá and oldest wife of Xangó, god of fire and thunder

The Orixás of Bahia

by Pierre Fatumbi Verger

The Bay of All Saints! It could also have been christened the Bay of All Orixás… Although the city of Bahia (the Bay) is famous for the opulence and number of its basilicas and cathedrals, its churches and convents, monuments that inspire the admiration of travellers and tourists, it is no less celebrated for being the place that, outside of Africa itself, is home to the most authentic centres of worship for the far-off Gods brought from other shores: Nagô Orixás, Dahomeyan Voduns, Angolan and Congo Inkissis.

The presence of these African religions in the New World is an unexpected consequence of the slave trade. The slaves were brought to various countries in the Americas and the Antilles, coming from different regions of Africa along the West Coast, between Senegambia and Angola. They also came from the opposite shore: the region of Mozambique and St Lawrence Islands, now Madagascar.

As a result, there came to the new world a mixture of captives who spoke various languages and had different customs and religions. All they had in common was the misery of being reduced to slavery, far from their homelands.

'Most favoured' relations were established between certain American and Caribbean countries and specific regions of the African conti-

Ceremony for the old Oxalá at the temple of Opô Afonjá

Waters of the great god Oxalá
(Ceremony of cleansing his body and soul by Xango)

nent: Bahia's relations were particularly strong with Angola and the Congo, until approximately the late 17th century. Later, the trade would shift to the East Coast of Castelo São Jorge da Mina, situated in the Bight of Benin, between the Volta and Lagos rivers. Such relations were later limited to the central part of that region – given the unfortunate name of the Slave Coast – demonstrating a marked preference for its most important port, called Glehué by the Dahomeyans, Igelefé by the Yoruba, Ajuda by the Portuguese, Judá or Grégoy by the French, Whydah by the English and Fidá by the Dutch.

Since the first days of the slave trade, in the 16th century, the presence of Bantus has been registered in Bahia. This group had a great influence on the Brazilian vocabulary. Later, a large number of Africans arrived from the regions inhabited by the Dahomeyans (Jéjé) and Yoruba (Nagô), whose rituals of worship seem to have served as a model for the ethnic groups already in Bahia.

For over three hundred and fifty years, the slave ships transported across the Atlantic not only the bodies of captives destined to work in the mines, cane fields, and tobacco plantations of the New World, but also their personalities, their ways of behaviour, as well as their beliefs.

The extraordinary resistance of these African

Yemanjá, goddess of the sea and waters; wife of Oxalá, gods of creation and parents to all the gods

religions to the forces of alienation and extermination which they frequently faced would have surprised all those who attempted to justify the cruel institution of slavery with the argument that their activities – those of the slavers – 'constituted the safest and most desirable means of bringing to the Church the souls of the blacks, which would be more advisable than leaving them in Africa, where they would be lost to degrading paganism or in danger of subjection to the heresies of foreign countries, to which they would be, at the very least, deplorably sent.' That is how the 'Businessmen of Bahia' expressed themselves in 1698 when they attempted unsuccessfully to establish a Company that proposed to build a fortress in Whydah in order to serve as a 'warehouse' for slaves awaiting shipment. Only twenty-three years later would the plan be realised due to the efforts of the Sea and War Captain José de Torres, established in Bahia de Todos os Santos.

Such was the concern with saving the Africans' souls from the hands of the heretics that in the late 18th century, Brazil went so far as to prohibit 'Protestant foreigners residing in Bahia from buying and owning blacks, particularly those newly arrived, in order to prevent the slaves from being inculcated with their errors and so that the Africans are not indoctrinated in any other but the true faith.' In Protestant countries, people held the same virtuous scruples and attempted to preserve these pagans from the perils of Papism. For the Moslems, the concern was the same: conducting these infidel idolators toward Arabia, Persia and Turkey so that they could be converted to the true faith – that preached by Mohammed...

Oxumaré, god of the rainbow, son of Oxalá and Naná

It can thus be seen that the slavers, professing a variety of forms of mono-theism, took great care to save the souls of the Africans, which were plunged in the gloom of idolatry.

In Bahia, all the Saints of Heaven were invoked to aid in this 'respectable' activity: the patron saints of slavers, their ships, and the merchandise they carried.

These very saints – the ones that had protected the interests of the slavers and the lives of some of the blacks being transported in their ships – had the good sense to perform an about-face after duly examining their conscience: they began protecting the slaves themselves, help-ing them to mystify their masters...

Perhaps they shared the belated remorse of Father Bartolomé de las Casas, who, with the pious intention of saving the lives of the Caraíba indians – an attempt that was ultimately fruit-less – began encouraging the trans-Atlantic slave trade in the 16th century. As a matter of fact, the trade between Africa and Europe had

already existed for some time. Spain and Portugal obtained a modest supply of Moorish and black slaves from northern Africa, along the Atlantic coast. The Berber states of North Africa did precise-ly the same thing, captur-ing the infidels (in this case, the Christians) and setting those 'dogs' to row on the benches of their galleys. In compensation, the holds of the Christian rulers' galleys were filled with Moors.

However, returning to the Saints of the Catholic Heaven, it is certain that they helped the slaves to fool and mislead their masters as to the nature of the dances the blacks were authorised to hold on Sundays, when they regrouped in *batuques* accord-ing to their nations of origin. In 1758, Count dos Arcos, the seventh Viceroy of Brazil, expressed his support for entertainments of this kind, not through philanthropy, but 'deeming it useful that the slaves retain the memory of their origins and do not forget the reciprocal feelings of animosity that led them to war against each other in the lands of Africa.' Thus divided, they would not attempt a joint rebellion (as they would do fifty years later) against their masters. These, seeing their slaves dance according to their customs and sing in their own languages, believed that this was nothing more than a pastime for nostalgic blacks. The masters actually had no idea that what was being sung dur-ing those meetings were actually prayers and praise

Ewá Gantois, the ancient goddess of divination

Procession for Oxún in the Opô Afonjá temple

for their Orixás, Voduns and Inkissis. When obliged to explain the meaning of their songs, the slaves declared that they were praising the Saints of Heaven in their own languages. Actually, they were invoking the aid and protection of their own gods.

It cannot be determined whether syncretism between the African gods and the Catholic saints already existed at that time, because the characteristics of the African divinities were still unknown to the slave owners and the Portuguese clergy in the 18th century, whereas the slaves were most likely ignorant of the details of the saints' lives.

It is difficult to identify the precise moment when this syncretism came to be established. It seems to be based, in general, on details of the saints' lives that could be compared to characteristics of the African gods.

It might seem strange that Xangó, the violent and virile thunder god, should have been compared to St Jerome, who is represented as a hairless old man, studiously bent over ancient books. However, in his images, the saint is frequently accompanied by a lion lying tamely at his feet. As the lion is a symbol of royalty among the Yoruba, St Jerome was compared with Xangó, their nation's third sovereign.

The connection between Obaluayé and St Lazarus is more evident, as the former is the god of smallpox and the body of the latter is represented as being covered with sores and abscesses.

Yemanjá, the mother of several other Orixás, was syncretised with Our Lady of the Conception, and Nanán Burukú, the oldest of the water divinities, was compared with St Ann, the mother of the Virgin Mary. Oyá-Yansan, the first wife of Xangó, divinity of winds and lightning, was identified with St Barbara. According to legend, the saint's father killed her because of her conversion to Christianity and was immediately hit by lightning and reduced to cinders.

The relationship between Christ Crucified and Oxalá, the divinity of creation, is the most difficult to explain, and may have arisen from the tremendous reverence and love that both inspired.

In Bahia, St George is identified with Oxossi, the hunter god, whereas in Rio de Janeiro he is syncretised with Ogun, the god of War. This is understandable in both cases, as St George is represented in engravings as a brave warrior in shining armour, mounted on a horse wearing a rich iron harness, which stamps the ground and prances. Armed with a lance, St George of Cappadocia kills a fearsome dragon – the favourite prey of the hunter god. To the great pleasure of the god warriors, 'in Rio de Janeiro, since the Empire, according to Arthur Ramos,

Obaluaé, god of the plague, infection and health

St George has appeared in processions mounted on a white horse with the honours of a colonel, reviewing the troops as he passes by.' In Bahia, however, Ogun is syncretised with St Anthony.

Baianas serving temple food

This connection between Ogun, the god of war, and St Anthony appears to be surprising, as the saint is generally depicted as having a sweet and charming disposition, carrying a lily in his hand and the Child Jesus in his arms. The key to the mystery of this strange association can be found in 'Reminiscences of Travels in Brazil' by Daniel Kidder, who writes that 'in 1595, a fleet left France under the command of a group of Lutherans with the intention of conquering Bahia. On the way, however, the Protestants attacked Argoim, a small island off the coast of Africa that belonged to the Portuguese. After practicing depredations of all kinds, they carried off, among other objects, a statue of St Anthony. As soon as they had set sail, they were assailed by a storm and lost several ships. Those who escaped the tempest were attacked by plague. During that calamity, out of hatred for Catholicism, they threw the image overboard after hacking at it with cutlasses. The ship that had carried it entered a port in Sergipe and all aboard were taken prisoner. When they were sent to Bahia, the first object they saw on the shore was the very image they had so mistreated!

'The Franciscans took the statue to their monastery in a procession… However, the friars were ashamed of its worn and ugly appearance, and set it aside in favour of a more pompous and elegant image… St Anthony was enlisted as a soldier in the fortress at the bay entrance, which bears his name. In that capacity, he received his pay regularly until he was promoted to the rank of Captain by Governor Rodrigo Costa on 16 July 1705. The procurator of the Franciscan monastery was authorised to receive a Captain's salary regularly in the saint's name.'

St Anthony was promoted to Major during the last World War. The Franciscan Friars keep a dress uniform that was offered to the saint by a wealthy devotee.

It seems that certain members of the Catholic clergy felt it convenient to encourage this syncretism, as Abbott Bouche suggested in Africa, when he described a statue of Iyangbá, the wife of Oxalá, in the following terms: 'This goddess is very similar to the Holy Virgin, as both are saviours of men.'

When linked to the African gods, the Catholic Saints become more understandable and familiar to the recent converts. It is difficult to ascertain whether this attempt made an effective contribution to converting the Africans, or whether it encouraged them to hide their true beliefs

Feast of Iansana, goddess of the wind

Festival of the sacred twins Ibeji

behind the shield of the saints. That question was put forth by Nina Rodrigues in 1890, at a time when syncretism between Orixás and Catholic saints was just beginning, and when the relationships between them varied from one terreiro to another. At that time, there was still a tendency to identify Xangó with St Barbara, as can be seen today in Cuba, despite the difference in sex. The argument that both were related to lightning seemed to dominate. Nina Rodrigues went on to say, 'Here in Bahia – as in all the missions to convert blacks in Africa, whether they be Catholic, Protestant or Moslem – rather than converting blacks to Catholicism, it is Catholicism that has been influenced by "fetishism", adapting itself to the animism... of the blacks.'

In order to understand this phenomenon, it is enough to attend a service in a Protestant church in Harlem, New York; or the ceremonies of numerous, more or less syncretic sects in Africa, such as that of the Cherubim and Seraphim, where the faithful are visited and possessed – often violently – by the Holy Ghost.

In the *candomblé* shrines, the two religions remain separate, and Nina Rodrigues noted that, at the time (the late 19th century), 'religious

Oia-Iansã

conversion did nothing more than juxtapose the very badly understood trappings of the Catholic rituals with their fetishistic beliefs and practices, which remained unchanged. They see their saints, or Orixás, and the Catholic saints as being equal, although entirely distinct from one another.

'The enslaved Africans declared themselves and appeared to be converted to Catholicism; they were able to maintain their fetishistic practices among themselves until today in almost as pure a form as in Africa.

'Later, constant voyages to Africa and direct shipping and commercial relations... facilitated the reimportation of these beliefs and practices, which might have been momentarily forgotten or adulterated.'

Over time, increasing numbers of people descended from Africans and mulattoes have been raised to respect both religions equally. As a result, they are as sincerely Catholic when going to church as they are attached to African traditions when zealously participating in the ceremonies of *candomblé*.

Edited and translated from *Os Deuses Africanos no Candomblé da Bahia*, 2nd edition, Editora Bigraf, Salvador, 1993

Pierre Verger

Holy Week,
Seville, Spain,
1935

It was perhaps my need for affirmation which brought me to Brazil, since I never did as I was supposed to. My father was a businessman who owned a fairly large factory which, theoretically, I was intended to take over. I worked there for a while with him, without exactly detesting the job. What complicated matters was the idea that I ought to pay an inordinate respect to *capital relationships*, to vested interests. Everything was directed towards forming *useful*, practical and commercial relationships.

This started from my earliest youth when, as a schoolboy before the Great War, I'd invite my classmates over to play of a Sunday. My father's first question was invariably: 'What profession does his father follow?' If I could answer that the boy happened to be the son of someone of importance, then I'd be told: 'Go on, invite him then!' If however, his parents belonged to a lower social stratum than mine, even if I wasn't aware of the fact, then the visit would prove 'unacceptable'. I was taught to admit only those who possessed hand-engraved visiting cards and to disdain those who bore only printed ones.

My father printed rather grander things than visiting cards: calendars, catalogues, posters. By the time I was twenty I began to realise that the prejudices I'd been imbued with were of little intrinsic value. I developed the tendency of

Watutsi, Kabgaye, Rwanda, 1951

doing the opposite of what was expected, in other words, of frequenting the company of those who in no way could be deemed 'useful'. I was lucky enough to fall in with good and interesting friends who opened up new horizons. In the early 30s, we were called *la bande à Prévert*, with the two Prévert brothers (Jacques and Pierre), Marcel Duhamel, Max Morize, Jean-Louis Barrault, Roger Blin and Maurice Baquet and their girl-friends. We met at the Rhumerie, then at the Café Flore. We formed a theatre company called *le groupe d'octobre* after the Russian [October] Revolution.

I myself didn't do too much theatre – though I think I took the only photographs – as I was exploiting the opportunity to travel. My mother passed on in 1932, which was a watershed for me, since as long as she was alive I felt obliged to retain a degree of bourgeois decency: my father and two elder brothers were dead and I was the only surviving member of the immediate family, although she was surrounded with her own – highly critical – brothers and sisters. I all but fell into Communism, deciding to go to the Soviet Union to celebrate the fifteenth anniversary of the Revolution. Doing so inevitably brought home the fact that contradicting family expectations was not the way to liberate oneself from them. Moscow was exciting and boring at the same time: a sense of futuristic optimism combined with long excruciating theoretical discourses. Having believed that what man became was conditioned by his environment, I gradually had to come to terms with the fact that each one of us possesses certain innate characteristics which determine the course of our lives.

Two months later, still reacting against the experience, I left for Tahiti – in search of Paul Gauguin, Pierre Loti … and the whole Pacific island idyll. I remained there a little over a year, compiling a book that was published in London [in 1937], called *South Sea Islands*. I never returned there. As soon as my mother passed on I took up my rucksack and set off for the Midi on foot, eventually completing 1500 kilometres around Corsica. That was the start of my compulsion for travelling, born of the remorse I felt at not belonging to the work ethic. My sense of sin could only be expiated by thirst, exhaustion and feet destroyed by walking.

That was why I left the Pacific, in flight from all that was familiar. The drama was that in the attempt to find the furthest point from civilisation I kept stumbling upon France. Papeete was another adjunct of my home, a totally French administration. Finally, in travelling from isle to isle by sailing boat, I reached Bora-Bora, now a tourist haven but then somewhere one reached without any idea of when the next boat would arrive to take you away. I intended to live in the hut of an indigenous man and the first thing I saw on entering it was a calendar on the wall, manufactured by my father. Inevitably, I was forever pursued by what I most sought to flee.

I've never managed to escape my past. It follows me, even in the shape of that calendar that so provoked me. At heart I've a great need for privation – and I've been fortunate enough to encounter it. At one point I even considered becoming a Buddhist monk, shaving my scalp so that no one would notice I'm balding, wearing a simple saffron-yellow toga, neatly fitting in. I encountered them in Cambodia, going out early to beg their daily bread, thereby performing a service to those who gave them rice and, in so doing, acquiring increased merit. It allows them to be beneficient while alleviated from the least care. What did bother me, however, was that this constituted the path to a good reincarnation, an egotistical aspect that displeased me and deviated me from my monkish goal. The desire to achieve a good reincarnation was not the privation I sought by renouncing all earthly desires. And I've so far failed in abandoning acquisitions by remaining attached above all to my books. Everything else, just about, has been sold, especially anything that made a noise: a radio, a gramophone, an electric fan. I don't have a kitchen and I eat what

I'm brought: my gravest concern is to ensure that my cat Jean-Jacques [Rousseau] is well fed.

In 1934 I contacted Marc Chadourne whose book on Tahiti had prompted me to go there, in the hope he might preface a new volume of my photos and that this, in turn, might attract the interest of a publisher. He received me courteously; he was interested; he agreed; he asked me to return in six months because in three days he was leaving for a trip around the world for *Paris-Soir*. As he reached the door to see me out, he enquired 'Why don't you come along too? I'm going with the journalist Jules Sauerwein and it'd be good to have someone along to take photos.' I went straight out and bought a Rolleiflex and some film. Three days later I departed to illustrate the features written by two great pre-War journalists. It was my luck that those came up in the wake of Colonel de la Roque's attempt to seize the Chamber of Deputies and people were envisaging another French Revolution. *Paris-Soir* was anxious to keep its best photographers at home – otherwise a staffer would undoubtedly have gone in preference to the unknown Pierre Verger.

The next piece of luck was that we ended up, having gone west around the world, at the *Paris-Soir* offices in London. That was where I learnt my pictures had been spiked. So I took them next door to the *Daily Mirror* and they spread my work across several pages. A poor layout but

the payment permitted me to undertake my first journey to Africa, and it allowed those of ill-will on *Paris-Soir* to discover just how bad a photographer this 'poor unknown' really was. I was then awarded a commission for a series on *Secret London*, with text by André Savignon, which liberated the fee I'd been promised on my return from the round-the-world voyage.

Ilave, Peru, 1942-44

Because the press was often so bad in its treatment of photographers a group of us formed the Alliance Photos agency at the end of 1934. Its five founders were Denise Bellon, Pierre Boucher, Emeric Feher, René Zuber and myself; all independent photographers, with Maria Eisner as picture editor to arrange commissions and payments. Later on [Robert] Capa joined us for news stories, and the advances certainly kept me alive until the War.

When War was declared I was mobilised, not without delay. Happily, in Mexico a thief had robbed me of my luggage – including my military papers – so that when I reported to the Consulate in Quito, where I happened to be at the time, the consul advised me: 'Ah well, carry on with your travels while we regularise your situation.' I continued on my way, being given the same advice at La Paz, Ascunción and Buenos Aires. Finally at Rio they were less understanding and sent me to Dakar. (All the French who found themselves on the eastern seaboard of Latin America were sent there; those on the west went to Martinique.) It was the happiest outcome possible, because that was how I came to know a certain Théodore Monod who became director of the French Institute in Africa and who later provided me with grants when I took up my study of African religions, there and in Brazil.

The fact that I already knew some Portuguese endeared me to the islanders off West Africa, the Cape Verdeans who understood my horrible mixture of Spanish and Portuguese which no other Frenchman would dream of attempting. They admitted me to a little bar they frequented in Dakar which, when curfew fell, became our home for the night. There in the blackout my bleached-out whiteness disappeared: I was no longer a white among blacks, since darkness denied all of us any colour at all. At last I needed to no longer feel ashamed of the lack of colour that had previously singled me out among people with whom I felt such a tremendous empathy.

On all the rest of my voyages to Africa, I was aware of remaining a white among blacks, whereas here my great love of Bahia stems from the excellence of its racial understanding. In Senegal a black is demonstrably different to a white. Here in Bahia there are so many shades of each, one is never sure where black ends and white begins. Even the very light-skinned participate in candomblé, experiencing no discrimination either way. There are no black ghettoes here and many blacks occupy positions of considerable prestige. For example, the women selling acarajés, the bean dumplings, on the street corners. Anywhere else in the world they'd be seen as negress street-sellers. Here they are individuals viewed with respect. You can tell by their lavish clothes they are 'daughters of a saint', that in candomblé ceremonies they are entered by the spirit of a god or goddess. People who visit one do so bent double in deference, whites as well as blacks, to kiss her hand before they take their acarajés, flattered by being permitted this contact with so eminent a personage.

This creates a legitimate sense of satisfaction among the blacks, knowing the respect they command. As for the rites of candomblé, they revolve around a black man or woman seated on a throne before whom all those attending come and prostrate themselves, placing their foreheads on the floor. Of course, receiving that kind of homage from blacks and whites alike, offsets any sense of resentment or humiliation between the races.

Before settling here I spent seventeen years in Africa, mainly in Benin (formerly Dahomey) and Nigeria. I was lost to photography when I began writing. I received two fellowships for a year apiece and my director of studies obliged me to write up my observations. When I protested: 'I'm a photographer not a writer!' I was told, quite sharply, 'Fine. No writing, no study grant.'

So I replied with an immense volume it took me 18 months to write, on the *Orixás*, the African gods.

My salvation was a lack of any working hypothesis. I was finally obliged to fall into the error of writing to explain things, explaining them the only way I could according to my temperament, just like everybody else. Since I really had no desire to explain anything at all I gathered all the available information haphazardly, without selecting material to support a specific hypothesis. So my second thesis had to link the *Orixás* to a sort of theory regarding psychological repression. It concerned what we call the state of possession by a god: a thoroughly awkward term of reference for crises of expression in the hidden and rejected sides of our unexpressed personality. Much of this I learnt through my own experience, helped by Lydia Cabrera, a remarkable anthropologist I came to know in Cuba.

What I also learnt was how the great monotheistic religions oppress their adherents, transforming them into guilty parties who must expiate the fact that one of our grandmothers gave an apple, a symbol of scientific knowledge, to Adam to munch. Therefore we – in my Cartesian culture, we Christians – are all sinful, with no right to happiness and only shame at being happy. Whereas in the African religions people express who they truly are: they can be inhabited by a violent god like Oxún or Ogun and there are those whose characteristics become invert-

Quang Ngai, Vietnam, 1938

ed, the men effeminate and the women masculine. Either way, there's no cause for reproach, since it's a god who inhabits the entranced person. Alas I can't go along with this explanation because I remain a Frenchman, with my own logic of the way things work.

None the less I have a particular part to play in these events. I first reached Bahia in 1946, and a very eminent woman, Dona Senhora, recited prayers over my head, consecrating me to Xangó. So when I visited Haiti and Cuba and, in 1948, Africa, I went with Xangó's red-and-white beads around my neck. When I reached Dakar I explained, 'I am a Xangó', showing my beads and was told, 'Good, then come to his temple.' There I was put through my paces, managing to make the correct responses, and was accepted as an adherent. Three weeks after arriving, I was invited to assist at a new offertory to Xangó and wanted to use my camera. Instead, I was obliged to deposit everything I'd brought and participate fully in the ceremonies, including dancing three times around the market place like a fresh initiate. This was important to the people there because the place was invaded by Catholic and Protestant missionaries, also an Islamic crusade, with nothing but contempt for African religions. My presence permitted them to announce: 'See, there *are* whites who practice this religion. It can't be as barbarian as all that.'

I was given the task of documenting the plants

Buenos Aires,
Argentina,
1941-42

they used, something which interested me not in the slightest. I ended up with around 3500 plants and 1500 scientific names: the rest were covered by being given different names according to their stages of growth and the combinations in which they were employed to work with others. Given my credulity, people came to me spontaneously with any number of samples. At first I thought they were sending me up: they kept arriving with the same species by another name. I was furious, they said anything to make fun of me, but then I was given a salutary lesson in linguistics. I learnt that there were formulae that needed to be uttered in order for the plant to function. The activating verb had to incorporate a syllable of the plant's Yoruba name. The syllable wasn't the name of the plant but of the verb: the plant had another name incorporating the relevant syllable. It was a different interpretation of language that was more interesting to me than simply the study of plants. Even so, it was hard not to become intrigued at the formulae and combinations used to create medicine guaranteed to heal recognisable illnesses and also to cure the crazy – or render others crazy…

My refusal to ask questions was as well since in doing so I would only have demonstrated my ignorance. It also put me in a different category to the anthropologists who arrive with their lists of enquiries. I became a student, learning what the people saw fit to teach me – and then returned to Paris to conduct seminars on what I'd learnt. I spent around ten years in Nigeria, travelling back and forth, and on my travels I encountered the books of Jorge Amado and then their author; I came to know [the singer] Dorival Caymmi and [the sculptor] Mario Cravo. I travelled and photographed to the tip of the northeast, then determined to settle in [Salvador de] Bahia. In 1953, I published a book on *The Influence of Bahia on the Gulf of Benin*, proving the reciprocal relations between Bahia and former Dahomey. Everywhere else under slavery the triangular trade had prevailed. Here there was a direct interchange of tobacco for slaves, tobacco being necessary to certain ceremonies, with Brazil and Cuba the sole suppliers.

I see myself as also something of a messenger, exchanging the memory of traditions and the practice of ancestral rites between two cultures. Why I'm not sure, only that my empathy goes right back to 1934 when a whole group of us from Museum of Ethnology [now the Museum of Mankind] went to the Bal Nègre on the Rue Blomet. There the chambermaids, the cooks, the valets from Guadaloupe and Martinique gathered out of sight of their damned bosses, forever swift to humiliate them if a lump of sugar appeared to have gone missing from the sugarbowl. That was where I first drank rum punch, danced in an explosion of joy worthy of a Brazilian Carnival, and discovered that exuberant gaiety which exists here. What's strange is that, also in 1934, I vowed never to write, observing the labours it created for Marc Chadourne who spent all his time taking notes and polishing phrases without a second's rest. Whereas for me, 'click', there was the image and once taken that was it, and I could move on to what came next.

So now I'm trapped: I don't write constantly, but I keep attempting to explain and rationalise even though at the end of it all I know there's no reason at all and nothing but false explanations, and that all my attempts can go to the devil. After all, I was brought up always to wear a hat in the street and to raise it whenever a lady passed by. To wear the same hat in a drawing-room would have shown me to be an ill-bred lout. As far as I'm concerned, this was a totally meaningless custom and to this day I still don't know why it arose. Fortunately this qualifies me as somewhat stupid and I don't attempt to raise clever questions and issues. Frequently people render themselves victims of the desire to demonstrate their intelligence, which inevitably leads to the opposite. Being without intellectual pretensions I can find that way of behaviour disastrous, attempting self-

validation by inviting the admiration of others.

As I said at the beginning: the need we all have for affirmation was fulfilled for me simply by coming to Bahia. And I've long since figured out that by far the most important thing in life is neither photography (which I gave up altogether around ten years ago) nor writing, but simply allowing myself to live and share with these people with whom I sustain so much empathy. I've begun to travel less, to appreciate existence more, even though I waste time terribly – like now, just stroking my corpulent [cat] Jean-Jacques – because before I wasted it terribly, simply wanting my existence to be over. I realise that after all I've grown slightly attached to my shell, perhaps through decreasing agility. I'm ninety-one years old, which is considerable when you consider I never wanted to reach forty, in order not to become an old idiot. Now I pretend to myself that I'm not, but from the age of thirty I took a length of cloth and cut off a millimetre a day until 4 November 1942, my fortieth birthday. Then, in reaching the end of the fabric, I reached the end of reading Yu Tang's *Importance of Life*. In so doing I failed my death and rediscovered existence.

Interview in Salvador, June 1993

Sikasso, Mali, 1936

Dona Senhora, Salvador, Bahia, 1946-62

Iawo, Ibualama, Salvador, Bahia, 1946-62

Bonfim, Salvador, Bahia, 1946-62

Salvador, Bahia, 1946-62

Bahia, 1946-62

Salvador, Bahia, 1946-62

Salvador, Bahia, 1946-62

Procession of Our Lord of Seafarers, Salvador,
Bahia, 1946-62

Sailboats, Olinda, Brazil, 1947

Salvador, Bahia, 1946-62

Bibliographies

Mario Cravo Neto
1947 Born in Salvador, Bahia

Selected individual exhibitions
1965 Galeria Convivium, Salvador
1971 Galeria Documenta, São Paulo
Museu de Arte Moderna da Bahia,
Salvador
XI Biennale Internacional de São
Paulo, São Paulo
1972 Galeria Grupo B, Rio de Janeiro
Galeria Documenta, São Paulo
1973 Galeria Documenta, São Paulo
XII Biennale Internacional de São
Paulo, São Paulo
1974 A Galeria, São Paulo
1975 XIII Biennale Internacional de São
Paulo, São Paulo
1976 Modern Art Galerie, Munich
1977 Galeria Multipla, São Paulo
XIV Biennale Internacional de São
Paulo, São Paulo
1979 Museu de Arte da Bahia, Salvador
(with Pierre Verger)
Museu de Arte de São Paulo, São
Paulo (with Pierre Verger)
1980 Foto Galeria, São Paulo
Galleria Il Diaframma, Milano
1981 Galleria La Parisina, Turino
Galeria Monica Filgueiras, São
Paulo
1982 Brazilian American Cultural
Institute, Washington DC
1983 Galleria Il Diaframma, Milano
Museu de Arte de São Paulo, São
Paulo
Arco Arte Contemporânea, São
Paulo
XVII Biennale Internacional de
São Paulo
1984 Museu de Arte Moderna, Rio de
Janeiro
Fotografia Oltre, Chiasso
1985 Yuen Lui Gallery, Seattle
IF – Imagine Fotografica, Milano
1986 Arco Arte Contemporanea, São
Paulo
1987 Vision Gallery, San Francisco
Billedhusets Gallery, Kopenhagen
1988 Suomen Valokuvataiteen Museo,
Helsinki
Palazzo Fortuny, Venezia
1989 La Galeria Kahlo – Coronel
Galeria O Cavalete, Salvador
Arco Arte Contemporanea, São
Paulo
1990 Galerie Springer, Berlin

Canon Image Centre, Amsterdam
1991 Galeria del Teatro General San
Martin, Buenos Aires
Ada Galeria, Salvador
1992 Houston FotoFest, Houston
Galeria Módulo, Lisboa
Fahey/Klein Gallery, Los Angeles
Witkin Gallery, New York
1993 Vision Gallery, San Francisco
Kathleen Ewing Gallery, Washington DC
Fisher Gallery – USC, Los Angeles
1994 Museum of Photographic Art, San
Diego
Frankfurter Kunstverein,
Frankfurt

Selected group exhibitions
1965 I Biennale de Artes Plasticas da
Bahia, Salvador
1971 V Exposição Jovem Arte
Contemporânea, Museu de Arte
Contemporânea de São Paulo
1972 Panorama da Arte Brasileira Atual,
Museu de Arte Moderna de São
Paulo
1975 Art Systems in Latin America,
Institute of Contemporary Art,
London – L'Espace Pierre Cardin,
Paris – Galleria Civica D'Arte
Moderna, Ferrara
1976 Arte Agora I, Museu de Arte
Moderna do Rio de Janeiro
1978 Subterranean Art, Architecture
and Objects, Galería Juan Martín
and Museo Carillo Gil, Mexico DF
Panorama 78, Museu de Arte
Moderna de São Paulo
1980 SICOF – Salone Internazionale
della Cinematografia, Ottica e
Fotografia, Milano
1981 Fotografia Lateinamerika,
Kunsthaus Zurich – Akademie der
Kunst, Berlin
Panorama 81, Museu de Arte
Moderna, São Paulo
1982 Biennale Internazionale di
Fotografia, Caserta
1983 Brazilian Photography, Six Contemporaries, The Photographer's
Gallery, London
Brésil des brésiliens, Centre
George Pompidou, Paris
1984 Photoamerica/84, Objettivi sull'
America Latina, Genova
Corpo e Alma, Espace Latino
Americain, Mois de La Photo, Paris

1985 I Quadrienal de Fotografia, Museu
de Arte Moderna, São Paulo
A Arte e seus Materiais – Atitudes
Contemporaneas, Galeria Sergio
Millet, Funarte, Rio de Janeiro
Panorama da Arte Atual Brasileira,
Museu de Arte Moderna de São
Paulo
50 Years of Color, Círculo de Bellas
Artes, Madrid
1986 Object Man, Portovenere
1988 Het Portret, Canon Image Centre,
Amsterdam
Brazil Projects, P S ONE – Institute
for Art and Urban Resources, New
York
Splendeur et misère du corps,
Museé d'art et d'historie de
Fribourg – Museé d'art Moderne
de La Ville de Paris
Triennale Internationale de La
Photographie – Mois de la Photo
1989 Réalités Magiques, Photografie
Latino Americaine Contemporaine, Museet for Fotokunst,
Odesen – Museum Voor
Fotografie, Antwerpen
1990 Von der Natur in der Kunst,
Messepalast Wien
Op Position, 2º Fotografie
Biennale Rotterdam
1991 13 Photographers, Witkin Gallery,
New York
Incursão pelo Imaginario na
Fotografia Brasileira Contemporanea, Rencontres Internationales
de la Photographie, Arles
1992 Arte Amazonas, Museu de Arte
Moderna, Rio de Janeiro
Staatliche Kunstthalle, Berlin
Encuentro de los Mundos, Museo
de Arte de la Tertulia, Cali
Arte America, Biblioteca Luis
Angel, Bogotá
America Latina, Vª FotoBiennale
de Vigo, Vigo
1993 Cartographies, Winnipeg Art
Gallery, Winnipeg, Canada

Books
Bahia, Raizes/Rhodia, São Paulo, 1980
Cravo, Aries Editora, Salvador, Bahia,
1983
A Cidade da Bahia, Aries Editora,
Salvador, Bahia, 1984
Os Estranhos Filhos da Casa, Aries Editora,
Salvador, Bahia, 1985

Ex Voto, Aries Editora, Salvador, Bahia, 1986
Mario Cravo Neto, exhibition catalogue, Idea Books, Milano, 1988
Mario Cravo Neto, exhibition catalogue, by Aries Editora, Salvador, Bahia, 1991

Cinematography
Ubirajara, directed by André Luis Oliveira, 35mm, feature, 1975
Smetak, directed by Walter Lima, 16mm, documentary, 1978
Nós, Directed by Walter Lima, 16mm, fiction, 1978
Iyá-mi-Agbá, The Secret Space, directed by Juana Elbain, documentary, 1979

Videos
GW-43, Gulf War, 20 minutes, 1990
Nash, U 19, Amazonia, 20 minutes, 1991
Exú dos Ventos, 15 minutes, 1992

Anna Mariani
1935 Born in Rio de Janeiro

Individual exhibitions
1972 Eucatexpo, São Paulo
1974 Enfoco, São Paulo
1979 Espaçonovo, São Paulo
1984 Arco, São Paulo
1988 Unicamp, São Paulo
     Centre de Création Industrielle, Centre Georges Pompidou, Paris
     FNAC/Forum, Paris
1989 Museum of Finnish Architecture, Helsinki
1990 Museu da Universidade Federal do Ceará, Fortaleza
     Charlottenborg Exhibition Hall, Copenhagen
     Institut für Auslandsbeziehungen, Stuttgart
     Haus der Kulturen der Welt, Berlin
     Arkitektskolen/Aarhus, Aarhus
1992 Centro de Convenções, Fortaleza
     Roberto Marinho Foundation, Rio de Janeiro
     Casa França-Brasil, Rio de Janeiro
     Museum of Contemporary Art, São Paulo

Group exhibitions
1980 Museum of Modern Art, São Paulo (Acquisition Prize)
1981 Kunsthaus, Zurich
1985 Panamerican Art School of São Paulo, São Paulo
     Museum of Modern Art, São Paulo
     Museum of Contemporary Art/Fotóptica, São Paulo
1987 19th São Paulo International Biennale – special room (Best Photographer of the Year Prize of São Paulo Art Critic Association APCA)
1988 PS1, The Institute for Art and Urban Resource, New York
     Staatliche Kunsthalle, Berlin
1989 Serpentine Gallery, London
     Stedelijk Museum, Amsterdam
1990 Fundação C Gulbenkian, Lisbon
1991 Museum of Contemporary Art, São Paulo
     Museum of Contemporary Art, Olinda

Photographic books
Pinturas e Platibandas, Rio de Janeiro, 1987
Façades (edition with french text), Rio de Janeiro, 1988
Paisagens, Impressões – O Semi-árido Brasileiro, São Paulo, 1992

Photographs published
Information, Copenhagen, March 1990
Contemporanea, Torino/New York, June 1989
The Independent Magazine, London, June 1989
Time Out, London, 27 June 1989
Valokuva, finnish photography, Nº4, Helsinki, 1989
Arkkitehti, Nº3, Helsinki, 1989
Helsingin Sanomat, Helsinki, 1989
Art in America, New York, January 1989
El Paseante, Nº11, Madrid, December 1988
Casa Vogue, Nº4, São Paulo, 1988
Summa, Buenos Aires, July 1988
The World and I, Washington, January 1988
Galeria, Nº6, São Paulo, October 1987
Veja, São Paulo, September 1987
Journal de Geneve, October 1987
Il Sole – 24 Ore, Milano, Febraury 1986

Video
Claudio Savaget, *The Semi-arid Region of Brasil by Anna Mariani*, 1992

Miguel Rio Branco
1946 Born in Las Palmas, Canary Islands

Individual exhibitions
1964 Paintings and drawings, Gallerie Anlikerkeller, Bern
1966 Paintings, Columbia University, New York
1967 Drawings, Galeria Relevo, Rio de Janeiro
1972 Experimental film and photography, Veste Sagrada, Rio de Janeiro
1974 Photographs, Galeria Grupo B, Rio de Janeiro
1977 Photographs, Ipanema Gallery, Tel Aviv
1978 Negativo Sujo [photomontages], Escola de Artes Visuais, Rio de Janeiro. Travels throughout Brazil
1980 Nada levarei quando morrer aqueles que mim deve cobrarai no inferno, Galeria Fotóptica, São Paulo. Travels to Fotogaleria Funarte, Rio de Janeiro
1982 Gabinete de Cultura, Bilbao
1983 Diálogas con Amaú, XVIIe Biennale de São Paulo, São Paulo
1985 Coeur miroir de la chair, Galerie Magnum, Paris
1986 Dialogues avec Amaú, Rencontres Internationales, Arles
1987 Coraçao espelho da carne, Fotogaleria Funarte, Rio de Janeiro
1988 Photographs, Palazzo Fortuny, Venice
1989 Paintings, Galeria Samarenha, Rio de Janeiro
1990 Multimedia exhibition, Photo Biennale, Rotterdam
     Drawings and paintings, Espaço Sergio Porto, Rio de Janeiro
1991 Audiovisual installation, Chappelle St-Jean de Moustiers, Rencontres Internationales, Arles
     Photographs, IFA Gallery, Bonn
1992 Städtische Galerie, Tuttlingen
     Fotogalerie Friedrichshain, Berlin

Group exhibitions
1965 Paintings, Sawdust Gallery, New York
1966 The Young Three, Sawdust Gallery, New York
1967 IXe Biennale, São Paulo
     Paintings, Salão Esso de Artes Plasticas, Rio de Janeiro
1968 Ephemeral objects and sculptures, Galeria Goeldi, Rio de Janeiro
1976 Grande São Paulo (photographs), Museu de Arte de São Paulo
1977 Photographs, Galeria Grafitti, Rio de Janeiro
1979 Nossa Gente (photographs), Fotogaleria Funarte, Rio de Janeiro
     Foto Bahia, Teatro Castro Alves, Salvador
1980 Camera Incantate (photographic installation), Palazzo Reale, Milan
     Quasi Cinema (film), Centro Internationale di Brera, Italy
     1st Photographic Triennale, Museu de Arte Moderna, São Paulo
1981 Quasi Cinema (installation and projection), Funarte, Rio de Janeiro
     Coleçao Gilberto Châteaubriand

(photographs), Museu de Arte Moderna, Rio de Janeiro and São Paulo
Coloquio Latino Americano de Fotografia (audiovisual projection), Mexico City
1982 Photographs, Kodak Centre, Paris
Contemporary Latin American Photography, Centre Georges Pompidou, Paris
1983 De l'eau dans le jazz, Rencontres Internationales, Arles
O tempo de olhar (photographs), Museu de Belas Artes, Rio de Janeiro, and Museu de Arte, São Paulo
Brésil des brésiliens, Centre Georges Pompidou, Paris
Sequences photographiques, Galeria Arco, São Paulo
1984 Photographs, 1st Art Biennale in Cuba, Havana
Les Présidents, Magnum Gallery, Paris
1985 Audio Retrato do Brasileiro, Museu de Arte Moderna, São Paulo
1986 1st Photography Quadriennale, Museu de Arte Moderna, São Paulo
On the Line, the New Colour Photojournalism, Walker Art Centre, Minneapolis. Travels to Portland, Oakland, Spencer, Laguna Museums of Art and the Carnegie Mellon Art Gallery
50 Jahre moderne Farbfotografie, Fotokina, Cologne
1987 Masters of Street photography III, Museum of Photographic Arts, San Diego, California
Latin American Photography, Australian Centre for Photography
1989 UABC, Contemporary Art in Uruguay, Argentina, Brazil, Chile (photographs), Stedeljik Museum, Amsterdam
3rd Biennale of Cuban Art (photographs), Havana
Rio Hoje (paintings), Museu de Arte Moderna, Rio de Janeiro
1990 Suadouro (photographs), Galerie 1900-2000, Paris
1992 Arte e Poder (photographic tryptichs), Paco Imperial, Rio de Janeiro
Brazilian Colour Photography, Houston Fotofest, Houston
5th Photo-Biennale, Vigo
Galerie Zeno X, Anvers
Arte Amazonas (audiovisual installation), Museu de Arte Moderna, Rio de Janeiro

Books
Dulce Sudor Amargo, Fondo de Cultura Economico, Mexico, 1985
Salvador de Bahia, Double Page, Paris, 1985

Prizes
1980 First Prize in the 1st Photography Triennale, Museu de Arte Moderna, São Paulo
1981 Prize for the best photography, Brazil Film Festival (for *Nada levarei…*)
1982 Special Jury Prize and International Critics' Prize, XI International Film Festival, Lille (for *Nada levarei…*)
Kodak Prize for Photography Criticism, Paris (with two others)
1986 Special Jury Prize in the International Festival of Short Films, Salvador, Bahia and Best Video Direction in the Festival of Film and Video, Maranhão (for *Apage-te, Sésamo*)
1988 Best photography for a full-length film, for *Memoria Viva*, directed by Otavio Bezerra and *Abolicão* by Zozimo Bulbul, Brasilia Film Festival

Luiz Figueiredo
1944 Born in Cuiabá, Mato Grosso, Brazil

Individual exhibitions
1966 Galeria Cosmo Velho, São Paulo
1976 Real Galeria de Arte, Rio de Janeiro
1977 Palácio do Catete, Rio de Janeiro
1978 Galeria Debret, Paris
1980 Galeria Bonfim, Amsterdam
1981 Brazilian Consulate, Berlin
Rotterdam Town Hall, Rotterdam
1982 Galeriá Gascón, Buenos Aires
Van Waning Gallery, Rotterdam
1983 Hotel Méridien, Island of La Réunion
1984 Galería Ramón Durán, Madrid
Galerie L'Oeil, Brussels
1985 Allende Centre, Rotterdam
Ibera Club, Bonn
UBP, Champs Elysées, Paris
1986 Sala Llorens, Barcelona
Voor Volkenkunde Museum, Rotterdam
Brazilian Embassy, The Hague
Croisière Paquet, Franco-Brazilian Project
1987 UBP, Place Vendôme, Paris
French Embassy, Brasilia
Galería Art Mojacar, Almería
1988 Galerie Art Naïf, Lasnes
Arturo López Cultural Centre,

Neuilly
1989 Galeria Bonino, Rio de Janeiro
1990 Museu Histórico do Rio de Janeiro, Rio de Janeiro
Museu de Artes e Tradicão Pop, Niterói
Museu de Artes Plásticas, São Paulo
Espaço Cultural de São Braz, Belem
Galeria Rômulo Mairona, Belem
Museu de Arte Contemporânea, Campinas
International Museum of Naïve Art, Rotterdam
Casa das Laranjeiras, Rio de Janeiro
Cidade Galeria, Angra dos Reis
1991 Galeria Bonino, Rio de Janeiro
1992 Galerie Debret, Paris
Galeria Bonino, Rio de Janeiro
1993 Durini Gallery, London

Group exhibitions
1966 Galeria Barcinsky, Rio de Janeiro
1967 Galeria Guignard, Belo Horizonte
1981 Paris Town Hall, Paris
Galerie des Nesles, Paris
1982 Charenton Town Hall, Charenton
1984 Jacovsky Museum, Nice
1986 French Cultural Centre, Abidjan
1990 Galeria Tina Zappoli, Porto Alegre
1991 Espace Michel Simon, Noisy Le Grand
Galerie t'Oude Raadhuys, Spijkenisse
Galerie de Waag te Brielle, Spijkenisse
1992 Musée d'Art Naïf Max Fourny, Paris

Salons
1966 Salão Mineiro de Artes Plásticas, Belo Horizonte
1982 Salon des Indépendents, Paris
1985 Salon des Indépendents, Paris
Café de la Paix, Paris
1983 to 1987 Artists Salon, Neuilly
1989 Salon Naïve Artists of Today, Jacovsky Museum, Nice
International Salon of Naïve Art, Unesco, Paris
1990 International Salon of 20th Century Art, Ghent
1991 Max Fourny Museum, Paris
International Salon of Humour, MAM, Rio de Janeiro
1992 Salon Comparaison, Grand Palais, Paris

Works in museums
International Museum of Naïve Art, Nice
Max Fourny International Museum of

Naïve Art, Paris
International Museum of Naïve Art, Vicq
Musée Vieux Chateau, Laval
Musée Daubigny, Auvers sur Oise
Sherbrooke Fine Arts Museum, Québec
Historic Museum, Rio de Janeiro
Plastic Arts Museum, Mooca, São Paulo
International Museum of Naïve Art,
   Rotterdam
International Museum of Naïve Art, Jaén

The bronze sculpture 'Serene Lady of
the Sea' inaugurated in 1988 in the
Praça dos Pescadores, Avenida Atlantica,
Rio de Janeiro, is by Luiz Figueiredo.

Carybé
1911 Born in Buenos Aires

Principal exhibitions
1944 Dibujos para Niños [Drawings for
        Children], to illustrate *Robinson
        Crusoe*, Consejo Nacional de
        Educación, Buenos Aires
1945 Scenes of America, Amauta
        Gallery, Buenos Aires
        Oils & Drawings, Amauta Gallery,
        Buenos Aires
1947 Agrupación Cultural Feminina,
        Salta (Argentina)
        New Work, Kraft Gallery, Buenos
        Aires
1948 Joint show, Artists of Argentina,
        Pan American Union, Washington
        DC
1949 With Gertrudis Chale, Viau
        Gallery, Buenos Aires
1950 Solo Show, Museu de Arte Moder-
        no, São Paulo and at Anjo Azul
        [night club], Salvador, Bahia
1951 Solo Show, Bureau de Educacão,
        Vitoria, Salvador
        1st Biennale, Museu de Arte
        Moderno, São Paulo
1952 Solo Show, Museu de Arte
        Moderno, São Paulo
        1st Brazilian Fashion Show [60
        models contributed], joint show
        promoted by Itamaraty in
        Switzerland and Holland
1953 With Mario Cravo, Teatro Santa
        Isabel, Recife, Pernambuco
        2nd International Biennale, São
        Paulo
1954 4th Fine Arts Exhibition, Salvador,
        Bahia
        Solo Show, Oxumaré Gallery,
        Salvador, Bahia
1955 3rd International Biennale, São
        Paulo
1956 28th Biennale, Venice
        Modern Artists of Bahia, Oxumaré
        Gallery, Salvador, Bahia

1957 Solo Show, Bonino Gallery,
        Buenos Aires
        Ibid, Bodley Gallery, New York
        6th Modern Art Salon, Rio de
        Janeiro
        Artists of Bahia, City Hall of Bahia,
        Salvador
        Nos e arte popular, Oxumaré
        Gallery, Salvador, Bahia
        Joint show, Museu de Arte
        Moderno, São Paulo
1958 Works by Brazilian Artists, Pan
        American Union, Washington DC
        and at San Francisco
        Solo Show, Bodley Gallery, New
        York
1959 30th International Exhibition,
        Seattle Art Museum
        Modern Artists of Bahia, Brazil/
        Portugal Exhibition, Salvador,
        Bahia
1961 Solo Salon, 11th São Paulo
        Biennale, São Paulo
1962 Solo Show, Museu de Arte
        Moderno da Bahia, Salvador
        11th National Modern Art Salon,
        Ministry of Education, Rio de
        Janeiro
1963 Solo Show, Bonino Gallery, Rio de
        Janeiro
        Brazilian Contemporary Artists,
        National Museum, Lagos
1964 Gallery of the Motion Picture
        Friends Society, São Paulo
        Solo Show, Villa Rica Gallery, São
        Paulo
        Christmas Exhibition, Querino
        Gallery, Salvador, Bahia
1965 Solo Show, Bonino Gallery, Rio de
        Janeiro
1966 1st National Plastic Arts Biennale,
        Salvador, Bahia
        Artists of Bahia, Hispanic Cultural
        Institute, Madrid
        Joint Show [Gulbenkian],
        Baghdad
        Joint show at Pietro Cortona
        Palace, Rome
        Holanda Gallery, Recife,
        Pernambuco
        Draftsmen of Bahia, Convivium Art
        Gallery, Salvador, Bahia
1967 Solo Show, Santa Rosa Gallery, Rio
        de Janeiro
1968 Bahian Artists, The Gallery, São
        Paulo
1969 Solo Show, Varig Airlines Office,
        London
        With Mario Cravo and Carlos Bas-
        tos, Portal Gallery, São Paulo
1970 Solo Show, Galeria da Praça, Rio
        de Janeiro
        Twelve Contemporary Brazilian
        Artists, Liverpool University,

Liverpool
1971 Orixá Panels, Museu de Arte
        Moderno, Rio de Janiero [plus
        tours Brazil]
        Special Room, 11th São Paulo
        Biennale, São Paulo
1972 Bahian Art Today, Hotel Miramar,
        Recife, Pernambuco
        50 Years of Modern Art in Brazil,
        The Gallery, São Paulo
1973 Jorge Amado and the Artists of
        Tereza Batista, Belo Horizonte
        12th Biennale, São Paulo
        1st Brazil/Japan Fine Arts
        Exhibition, Tokyo [plus Japan/
        Brazil tour]
1974 1st Art Salon, Engineering Club of
        Bahia, Salvador
1975 2nd Art Exhibition Brazil/Japan
        [plus Japan/Brazil tour]
        8 Bahian Artists, Belo Horizonte,
        Minas Gerais
1977 3rd Fine Art Exhibition Brazil/
        Japan [plus Japan/Brazil tour]
        3rd Plastic Arts National Congress,
        State Bank, Brazil
1979 Joint exhibition in the 'Catacomb
        Park', Rio de Janeiro
1980 Bahia Week, Cassino Estoril,
        Lisbon
        Bahian Painters, Dakar
        13th Contemporary Art Exhibit-
        ion, Chapel Art Club, São Paulo
1982 Afro-Brazilian Week, Porto Alegre,
        Rio Grande do Sol
        Three Artists from Bahia, Thomas
        Jefferson House, Brasilia
1983 The Iconography of African Gods
        in Bahia's Candomblé, Caribbean
        Cultural Centre, New York
        Joint show, Brazilian American
        Cultural Institute, Washington DC
1984 Solo Show, Museo Nacional de las
        Culturas, Mexico City
        Solo Show, Philadelphia Arts
        Institute, Philadelphia
        Artists of Bahia, Edson Queiroz
        Foundation, University of Fort-
        aleza, Ceará
1985 Bahian Art, 2000 Gallery, San José
        de Costa Rica
        Solo Show, Escritorio de Arte da
        Bahia, Salvador, Bahia
1986 39 Drawings from the Recôncavo
        Collection, Salvador, Bahia
        Retrospective 1936-1986, Desen-
        banco Arts Centre, Salvador, Bahia
        Solo Show, Cassino Estoril Gallery,
        Lisbon
1987 Bahian Modernists, Museu de Arte
        Moderno, Salvador, Bahia
1988 Retrospectiva, Buenos Aires

Books

Since 1940, Carybé has painted murals and ceilings, designed theatre and dance sets and costumes, and published books and illustrations almost annually. His principal publications include those to:

Poems by Walt Whitman, Schapiro, Buenos Aires, 1944

Uncle Tom's Cabin by Harriet Beecher Stowe, ibid

Robinson Crusoe by Daniel Defoe, Viau, Buenos Aires, 1945

Ajtuss, pictures and text by Carybé, Botella al Mar, Buenos Aires, 1948

The Middle San Francisco by Wilson Lins, Oxumaré, Salvador, 1952

The Yellow Butterfly by Rubem Braga, José Olympio, Rio de Janeiro, 1953

The Turban of the Bahian Woman and *The House of the Rose* by Carlos Vasconcelos Maia, Bahia State Museum, Salvador, 1955

Macunaima by Mario de Andrade, Society of the Bibliophiles of Brazil, 1957

Ali Baba and the 40 Thieves, Rola RSL, Buenos Aires, 1959

The King of the Mountains, The Vanguard Press, New York, 1960

Carybé, Portfolio in 'Masters of Drawing' Collection, Cultrix, São Paulo, 1961

The Seven Doors of Bahia, Livraria, Salvador, 1962

Bahia, the Good Land Bahia, with Jorge Amado and Flavio Damm, Imago, 1966

Capoeira Angola by Waldemar Rego, Itapoa, Salvador, 1968

Nobody Writes to the Colonel by Gabriel García Márquez, Sabia, Rio de Janiero, 1969

Brazilian by Flavio Roiter, Atlantis, Zurich, 1969

The Burial of the Devil; The Funeral Rites of Big Mamma; 100 Years of Solitude, all by Gabriel García Márquez, Sabia, Rio de Janiero, 1970

The Green House by Mario Vargas Llosa, Sabia, Rio de Janiero, 1971

Portfolio of Drawings of Nureyev's Ballet, Sabia, Rio de Janiero, 1972

Candida Erendira and her Wicked Grandmother by Gabriel García Márquez, Record, Rio de Janiero, 1973

The Spotted Cat and the Lady Swallow by Jorge Amado, Record, Rio de Janiero, 1976

Springtime Speech and Some Shadows by Drummond de Andrade, Record, Rio de Janiero, 1977

Seven African Legends of Bahia, Portfolio for Onile, Salvador, 1979

Iconography of the African Gods in Bahia's

Candomblé, Ralzes, São Paulo, 1981

African Legends of the Orixás by Pierre Verger, Corrupio, Salvador, 1985

The War of the Saints by Jorge Amado, Record, Rio de Janiero, 1988

Pierre Verger
1902 Born near Paris, France

Pierre Verger has 65,000 extant slides/negatives in his own collection. His publisher-friend Paul Hartmann published the French editions of his photographic books. After 1953, Verger concentrated on botanical and ethnological publications in which his photographs illustrated his own writings. Since 1980, the baiano publishing house Corrupio have been responsible for issuing his work in Brazil.

Books and publications
* articles/theses

En Espagne, text by M Legendre, Paul Hartmann, Paris, 1935

Italie, des Alpes à Sienne, text by J L Vaudoyer, Paul Hartmann, Paris, 1936

South Sea Islands, text by R Condon, Routledge & Sons, London, 1937

Au Méxique, introduction by J Soustelle, Paul Hartmann, Paris, 1938

Fiestas y Danzas en el Cuzco y en Los Andes, Editorial Sudamérica, Buenos Aires, 1945

Incas of Peru, Pocohontas Press, Chicago, 1950

Brésil, with A Bon and M Gautherot, introduction by A Lima, Paul Hartmann, Paris, 1951

Congo Belge, text by C d'Ydewalle, Paul Hartmann, Paris, 1952

L'Influence du Brésil au Golfe du Bénin, Mémoire 27 d'IFAN, Dakar, 1953

Le Japon, entre la tradition et l'avenir, text G Duhamel, Mercure de France, 1953

Dieux d'Afrique, Paul Hartmann, Paris, 1954

Bahia de Tous les Poètes, Guilde du Livre, Lausanne, 1955

Première Cérémonie d'initiation au culte des Orishá Nago à Bahia, Brésil, Revista do Museu Paulista, Vol IX, São Paulo, 1955*

Indiens pas Morts, Delpire, Éditions Hoa Qui, Paris, 1956

Haiti, la terre, les hommes et les dieux, Editions Baconnerie, Neuchâtel, 1957

Notes sur le Culte des Orishá et Vodoún à Bahia, la Baie de tous les Saints au Brésil et sur l'ancienne Côte des Enclaves, Mémoire 51 d'IFAN, 1957*

Cuba, Paul Hartmann, Paris, 1959

Grandeur et décadence du culte de Iyami

Osoranga (Ma mere la sorcière) chez les Yoruba, Journal de la Société des Africanistes, Vol 35, Paris, 1965*

The Yoruba High God, University of Ife, Ile-Ifé, Ibadan, 1966

Les Côtes d'Afrique Occidentale entre Rio Volta et Rio Lagos (1515-1773), Journal de la Société des Africanistes, Vol 38, Paris, 1968*

Flux et Reflux de la traité des nègres entre le golfe de Bénin et Bahia de Todos os Santos, Thèse de 3 cycle, Mouton, Paris, 1968*

Trance et Convention in Nago-Yoruba Spirit Mediumship in Africa, London, 1969

Automatisme verbal et communication du savoir chez les Yoruba, L'Homme, Vol XII, Paris, 1972*

Trade Relations between the Bight of Benin and Bahia, Ibadan University Press, Ibadan, 1976

Retratos da Bahia, Editora Corrupio, Salvador, 1981

Lendas dos Orixás, illustrated by E Guerra, Editora Corrupio, Salvador, 1981

Noticias da Bahia, Editora Corrupio, Salvador, 1981

Oxossi o Caçador, illustrated by E Guerra, Editora Corrupio, Salvador, 1981

Orixás, Deuses lorubas na Africa e o novo Mundo, Editora Corrupio, 1981

Orishá, les dieus Yorouba en Afrique et au nouveau Monde, Editions A-M, Métalié, Paris, 1982

50 anos de Fotografia, Editora Corrupio, Salvador, 1982

Lendas africanas dos Orixás, illustrated by Carybé, Editora Corrupio, Salvador, 1985

Flux e Refluxo do Tráfico de Escravos entre o Golfo de Bénin e a Bahia de Todos os Santos, Editora Corrupio, Salvador, 1987

Centro histórico de Salvador, Editora Corrupio, Salvador, 1989

Pierre Verger, photographies, Editions du Désastre, Paris, 1989

Pierre Verger, la Messager/The Go-Between, Photographies 1932-1962, Editions Bleu Outremer Revue Noire, Paris, 1993

Films

Les Mollécules Sacrées, film by Jean Lalier and Monique Toselo, ORTF, Paris, 1971

Africains du Brésil et Brésilens d'Afrique, film by Yannick Bellon, ORTF, Paris, 1975

Les Orishás, film by Monique Toselo, TV2, Paris, 1985

A tun pade, video by José Guerra, Corrupio, 1989

Afterword

Brazilian Contemporary Arts [BCA] is proud to be supporting the artists and photographers described in this book, presented in a major London exhibition as a highlight of BCA's 1994 Festival of Bahia.

BCA, founded at the start of the 1980s as a charity, has won a special place in the hearts of everyone in Britain who is interested in the culture and arts of Brazil. Its launch was an act of audacity by a German, the late Horst Troege, who at that time was a finance officer at the ICA (Institute of Contemporary Arts – hence BCA's own name). Its survival and development has, to those closely involved, seemed sometimes miraculous.

Troege had fallen in love with Brazil and, helped by his Brazilian wife Cecilia, arranged a three week season of films, lectures and other events at the ICA in 1981. It was called 'In Floodlight – Brazil'. He guaranteed this out of his own pocket and, perhaps to his own surprise, found he was only £200 out at the end.

Encouraged by Professor Leslie Bethell, myself and others, BCA became properly established and in 1983 launched a far more ambitious two month festival in venues throughout Britain – with dance, music, visual arts, films and lectures. It made an impact but it also made an almost crippling loss. Since the mid-eighties, when Troege moved to Brazil, Edna Crepaldi has worked hard as our second director, with a devoted band of helpers, to nurse BCA to its present state of artistic and financial health.

There have been many landmarks. BCA has brought a wide range of musicians here, from Gilberto Gil to Marisa Monte; art exhibitions, such as the Châteaubriand collection which BCA was instrumental in bringing to the Barbican in 1984; and films not otherwise available. It has run regular dance and carnival events. Its consultancy for the Gulbenkian Foundation helped to establish Portugal 600 (the Anglo-Portuguese Foundation which is the key Portuguese arts body in Britain). It took a leading role in the 1989 celebrations of the Centenary of the Brazilian Republic.

And, as an arts educational charity, it has steadily pursued less glamorous aims. Its newsletter reaches thousands. It offers language classes, dance classes, lectures and discussions on arts and social topics. It has gained increasing commercial sponsorship and, over the last few years, direct financial assistance as well as valuable goodwill from the Brazilian Embassy in London. It is attracting new members all the time.

We hope that in enjoying this book and the exhibition you will have been inspired to attend other events in the current Festival of Bahia. If you want to know more about the lively arts of Brazil, BCA is at your service.

Richard Bourne
BCA Council